My Bro

Letters to a Younger Brother
on the
Virtues and Vices
Duties and Dangers of Youth

JAMES W. ALEXANDER

SOLID GROUND CHRISTIAN BOOKS
BIRMINGHAM, ALABAMA USA

SOLID GROUND CHRISTIAN BOOKS
2090 Columbiana Rd., Suite 2000
Birmingham, AL 35216
(205) 443-0311
sgcb@charter.net
http://solid-ground-books.com

MY BROTHER'S KEEPER:
Letters to a Younger Brother on the Virtues and Vices, Duties and Dangers of Youth

by James Waddel Alexander (1804-1859)

First published in 1838 by The American Sunday School Union, Philadelphia, PA

American Sunday School Union Classic Reprint

ISBN: 1-932474-66-8

Cover Design by Borgo Design, Tuscaloosa, Alabama
Contact them by e-mail at nelbrown@comcast.net

Cover image taken from the original work published by the American Sunday School Union, engraving by J.B. Neagle (See Chapter 2, pp. 7-14)

Manufactured in the United States of America

Preface to New Edition

"Am I my brother's keeper?" These words have become the mark of Cain for thousands of years since they were first uttered. He has been set forth from the beginning as the pre-eminent example of ungodliness in brotherly relations.

James W. Alexander (1804-1859) was the first-born son of Archibald and Janetta Alexander. This book is clear proof that he took seriously his position in the family. Each of the twenty-one chapters in this book is a letter that was originally written and sent to his youngest brother. It is crystal clear that Alexander embraced his role to be his brother's keeper, and hence the title of this volume.

J.W. Alexander was a brilliant man who loved his Lord and devoted his life in the spirit of Ezra, of whom we are told, *"For Ezra had set his heart to study the law of the LORD and to practice it, and to teach His statutes and ordinances in Israel"* (Ezra 7:10). Study—practice—teach. This is the open secret of the usefulness of this man. This is the open secret for usefulness of all mankind.

This book was first published in 1838 by the American Sunday School Union, an organization supported by Alexander throughout his entire ministry. It was intended to reach down to young men at an age before their habits were already fully formed. It is filled with page after page of sage advice appropriate for those ten years old and above. No one who cares about eternity will read this in vain.

Ever since this publisher was privileged to bring back into print *Thoughts for Young Men* by J.C. Ryle (in 1990), he has searched for another volume to rival and supplement that brilliant book. This is, at long last, that volume. May the Lord of the harvest use this book to rescue many young men from the precipice of a Christ-less eternity! *Soli Deo Gloria!*

The Publisher
Christmas 2004

Table of Contents

Letter 1 —	Reading the Scriptures	1
Letter 2 —	Gratitude to Parents	6
Letter 3 —	Life is Short	15
Letter 4 —	Holidays	19
Letter 5 —	Amusements	23
Letter 6 —	Bodily Exercise	29
Letter 7 —	Early Rising	34
Letter 8 —	The Habit of Diligence	41
Letter 9 —	Learn Something Every Hour	48
Letter 10 —	Three Self-taught Scotch Lads	56
Letter 11 —	Formation of Habits	63
Letter 12 —	Dangers of Evil Companions	68
Letter 13 —	Friendships	74
Letter 14 —	Good Example	80
Letter 15 —	Truth and Falsehood	86
Letter 16 —	Manly Independence	91
Letter 17 —	False Shame	95
Letter 18 —	Evil Speaking	100
Letter 19 —	Benevolence	105
Letter 20 —	Secret Prayer	111
Letter 21 —	The Great Concern	116

Letter 1

Reading the Scriptures

My dear brother,

You gave me much gratification when you informed me that you were attentive to the reading of the Scriptures. And I rejoice to find you inquiring how you may continue to read them with greater profit. I shall answer your questions, and shall also, from time to time, write you some directions on other things; such as your learning, your manners, and your amusements. I take your questions as you ask them.

1. Ought I to read the Bible in regular order?

I think you ought. Not that this should be the only way of reading: but every day you should be going forward. Suppose you were roaming through a beautiful estate, such as the place on the Delaware where Joseph Bonaparte resides; and that your object was to learn all about it. You might pursue *two* methods. *First,* you might set out at one of the gates, and follow the first path, then strike off into a grove, and walk a few steps; then branch into a garden; then return to see the fishpond or the statue. You might spend a day or two in this employment, and at the end of it you would have seen a great many beautiful things. But while you had looked at some of these four or five times over, there would be a great number of spots which you had not seen at all. Instead of looking ten times at the observatory, you might have looked at ten different scenes. What was the matter? I will tell you; you did not view it in *regular order.* You had no plan. So you might spend years in reading the Scriptures; and at the end of them, you would have learned many whole chapters or even books of the Bible; yet there might be some very useful parts which you would know nothing about. Why? Because you did not read in *regular order.*

Secondly: You might get an exact plan of Bonaparte's grounds, like a little map, on a piece of paper; then you might divide it off into portions, and say, "I can do so much today, and so much tomorrow, &c." Then you might go over every step of the fine park and gardens, look at every bridge, and examine every curiosity. You would have surveyed every single beauty. But what makes the difference between these methods? You viewed it this second time in *regular*

Letter 1 — On Reading the Scriptures

order. Thus, too, you ought to read the Scriptures. And if you lay down a plan, and take care to observe it, and keep it up for a few years, you will know something about the whole Bible. Why? Because you read it in *regular order.*

2. Ought I to commit verses to memory?

Most certainly you ought; at least half a dozen every day. The more you learn by rote, the more you will be able to learn.

If you get six verses every morning, for one year, you will have learned more than two thousand verses, or more than sixty chapters.[1] But this is not all. At the end of the year, it will be as easy for you to commit twenty verses to memory, as it is now for you to commit half a dozen. The best plan I know of is to learn your verses partially just before you prepare to go to bed. Think of them as you are falling asleep, repeat them as you wake the next morning; and after your morning devotions, learn them perfectly. This you will find, when you go further in your Latin, was the advice of the ancients, and if you lay to heart what you learn, it will be the greatest treasure. Nobody can rob you of it. You may he shipwrecked, or robbed, or

---

[1] Publisher's Note: The counsel given by Alexander appears to be overwhelming to modern ears, but it is nothing more than he had done himself when he was younger. Rather than reject this advice out of hand, let the reader put this to the test.

imprisoned, but no one can take this out of your memory.

3. *Ought I to read the Bible for amusement?*

Not exactly. If you mean reading it with a thoughtless, careless mind, certainly not. But if you mean, reading its beautiful narratives, and its lively descriptions, because you admire them, and because it refreshes and delights you, certainly it is right for you to read it thus. I have just been reading again the story of Joseph, in the book of Genesis, and I find it more charming than any thing I ever saw in any history or romance. Now there is no harm in your going to the Bible for pleasure, rather than to any other book. It is remarkable that more persons do not find out how much interesting history the Scriptures contain. Just think of the life of David. It is far more striking than that of Peter the Great,[2] or Baron Trenck.[3] Yet scarcely any one opens the Bible to find rational entertainment.

So I have answered your questions: and now I shall add a few remarks of my own. There are two books in the Bible which are exceedingly interesting and useful. One was written in poetry; the other in prose. The greater part of one was composed by a great king; the greater part of the other by his son, another

---

[2] Peter Alexeevich (1672-1725) was both Czar and Emperor of Russia.
[3] Baron Frank Trenck (1711-1749), was born in Italy and later became known for his exploits on the battlefield.

Letter 1 — On Reading the Scriptures

great king. One was by a warrior, a musician, and a poet; the other was by the wisest monarch who ever lived. In these two books you will find directions for your *devotions* and your *conduct.* The Psalms are noble pieces of prayer, thanksgiving, and praise; the Proverbs are short sayings, every one of which is full of meaning, and rich with wisdom. When you are older, I would recommend to you to read each of these books through *once a month.* The book of *Psalms* is already divided into portions, for every morning and evening, in the book I gave you. And the book of *Proverbs* has just as many chapters as there are days in the long months, one for every day. Scarcely any day will pass in which you will not find an opportunity to govern your speech or your behavior by some one of these short maxims. And as the Lord Jesus Christ is the great *subject of* many psalms, you will learn from the New Testament how to find him everywhere in your daily reading.

Farewell, my dear boy. Attend to your studies and your health, and, above all, offer up your heart to God.

I am your affectionate brother,

James

Letter 2

Gratitude to Parents

My dear brother,

I wrote you on this subject thus early in my course of letters, because I think gratitude to parents is the foundation of a great many virtues; and one of the first and most distressing symptoms of a decline from the paths of virtue is the unkind or contemptuous treatment of parents. The first commandment with promise is the command to honor our parents, and our earliest duties are those which we have to render to our father and our mother. You will find counsels on this subject scattered through my letters; but as young people are apt to be impressed by narrative, I will give you a little history, which I am sure you will find interesting. The story is connected with the beautiful engraving on the cover of these letters.

Letter 2 — Gratitude to Parents

There lived two poor men in a very rough and mountainous country, where they kept their flocks, and cultivated such little spots of earth as they could find among the rocks and crags. It was a region abounding in rapid streams, which poured in torrents from the precipices. There was scarcely any point from which you might not see the tops of mountains covered with snow. The hills were so rough that it was difficult and dangerous to travel even a mile, from one hamlet to another. Carriages were almost unknown, and most of the inhabitants traveled on foot, and carried their goods upon mules or asses.

Ulrich and Godfrey, the two men I have spoken of, had large families, and in each of these was a little boy about eleven years of age. These boys often played together, but they were exceedingly unlike in temper. Little Ulrich was sullen and rude; while his playmate Godfrey was kind and gentle. Ulrich's mother found it very hard to manage the stubborn little boy. He was undutiful and unkind, and gave his parents many hours of anxiety. Sometimes when he was sent to look for the cattle, which strayed in the mountains, he would go to some of the neighbors' houses, and stay several days, while his mother would be in the greatest alarm, lest some accident had befallen him. The ungrateful boy seemed never to think of what might be the cares of his parents. He did not reflect on the hours and days and months of solicitude which his poor mother had felt on his account; how she had watched by his pillow when he slept, and nursed him when he was sick, and provided his food, and sat up many a long night to make or mend his clothes. Forgetful of all this, Ulrich would be sulky and sour when she spoke to him, and would even reproach her in the harshest and most inappropriate language.

Little Godfrey was just the reverse of all this. He loved his parents most tenderly, and delighted to obey them in every particular. Consequently he was far happier himself, and made all around him happy.

One afternoon, Ulrich's mother had directed him to do some little piece of work which was not quite agreeable to him, and the bad boy as usual flew into a passion, and called his mother several hard names. The poor woman wept as if she would break her heart, but this only made him rage more furiously. At last, giving his mother a look more like that of a wild beast than a son, he dashed out of the house, muttering to himself that he would never return again. This was as foolish as it was wicked, for the silly child had no place where he could live for any length of time; and he might have known that his father, whose temper was as violent as his own, and who was often in drink, would soon drag him back home, besides chastising him. But people in

Letter 2 — *Gratitude to Parents*

a passion seldom stop to consider, and Ulrich hastened away, and began to ascend one of the steep mountain paths. As he advanced, his mind was drawn away, by degrees, to other thoughts. At one moment he would pause to examine the scanty flowers which peeped out from among the rocks; at another, he would stand and listen to the distant waterfall, or the hunter's rifle; and then he would be attracted by the circling flight of the Alpine eagle. Amidst these thoughts his conscience began to whisper to him, "Ulrich, Ulrich, you are a wicked boy! You are breaking the heart of your affectionate mother! Go back, go back!"

As Ulrich sat by a tall cliff, looking westward to where the sun was going behind a range of blue mountains, he thought he heard voices in the winding path above him. "I think I know that voice," said he; "it must be old Father Simon, coming down the valley. Poor old man! I wonder that he does not fall and break his neck among these sharp crags." I ought here to mention, that Father Simon was a very aged man, more than eighty years old, who used to travel about the mountains with the aid of a little dog; the faithful animal ran before, with a little bell at his collar, and the old man, who was totally blind, felt his way with a long staff, and held a string which was fastened around the dog's neck. But on the day I have mentioned, the poor little dog had been disabled by a large stone which fell upon his back from one of the crags, and Father Simon was forced to sit down and wait some hours for assistance. It was indeed his voice which Ulrich heard, but to whom was he speaking? Ulrich listened, and soon perceived that it was a child's voice, and a moment after, as the blind man came into sight, by turning a corner, Ulrich saw that he was guided by his playmate, little Godfrey. "Step this way, Father Simon," said the kind little boy, as he helped the poor old man along. "Now lean on my shoulder, and put your right foot down into this hollow." "May Heaven reward you, my dear boy," said the old man; "happy are the parents who have such a son. My poor sightless eyes cannot behold your face, but I hear the gentle tones of your voice. I am weary; let us rest for a few moments here, where the ground seems level." So saying, Father Simon slowly bent his aged limbs, and sat down by the side of a rock. At the same moment Godfrey recognized his neighbor Ulrich, who was seated a few paces off, and whom he was delighted to meet.

I have said that Ulrich was in no very pleasant state of mind. Conscience was piercing him for his filial ingratitude; and, at such a moment to see his friend Godfrey engaged in an act of kindness made him feel still more guilty. He could not help saying to himself, "See what Godfrey is doing for that old man.

Letter 2 — *Gratitude to Parents*

He is kinder to a poor stranger than I am to my own mother. Indeed, I must be a very wicked boy." As these thoughts passed in his mind, he drew near to the others, and Godfrey told Father Simon that this was one of his friends and playmates. "Well, my children," said Father Simon, "if you will rest with me here for a short time, I will try to say something to you which may be useful. This little boy has been very kind to a poor old blind man; he has perhaps saved my life, for since I have lost my Argus, I have no friend left, and I might have lain and perished on the mountain. My child, God sees and approves such conduct, and he will reward it. The command of God is, *'Thou shalt rise up before the hoary head, and honor the face of the old man.'*[4] I hope you remember what became of the youth who cried after an old prophet, 'Go up, thou bald head!'[5] When I find a child who is very kind to poor and aged persons, I feel sure that he is affectionate and obedient to his parents."

Ulrich felt very badly when he heard this, for it seemed as if the old man had known what was passing in his mind. Father Simon went on to say: "I often say these things to young people, because I remember with sorrow many things I might have done for my parents when I was a child; and I think of them the more

---

[4] Leviticus 19:32.
[5] 2 Kings 2:23.

because Providence has left me in my old age without son, or grandson, to take care of me. Children, mark my words: if you desire to lead happy lives, obey your parents; love them, honor them, and serve them. Never let the evil one tempt you to give them a harsh word or an angry look."

Little Godfrey looked up, and said, "Father Simon, I think none but a very wicked boy could be cross to his dear father and mother." Ulrich's face became as red as crimson at these words, because he knew that he was just such a boy. Father Simon went on to say: "If you wish to make your parents happy in their old age, take pains to please them in every way. *'A wise son maketh a glad father; but a foolish son is the heaviness of his mother.'*[6] They are the best friends you can ever have in this world; never let your conduct give them pain. *'A foolish son is a grief to his father, and a bitterness to her that bare him.'*[7] When parents become old and weak, their greatest comfort is in their children; be sure to attend to their wishes. *'Hearken unto thy father that begat thee, and despise not thy mother when she is old.'*[8] For if you should grow up in wickedness, and treat your parents with contempt, you will fall under that awful curse: *'The eye that mocketh at his father, and despiseth to obey his mother, the*

---

[6] Proverbs 10:1.
[7] Proverbs 17:25.
[8] Proverbs 23:22.

Letter 2 — Gratitude to Parents

ravens of the valley shall pick it out, and the young eagles shall eat it.[9] The whole course of God's providence will be as much against you, as if the birds of prey which you see every day in these mountains were to turn against you, and tear you with their talons."

Here the old man, being somewhat rested, arose, and taking Godfrey's hand, proceeded on his way. Ulrich sat still under the rock; he was agitated and alarmed, so that his limbs trembled. At length he suddenly arose, and said to himself, "I will go back to my mother." He quickened his steps, as he saw that night was coming on, and soon reached his father's cottage. As he went along, he thought a great deal about what he should say to his offended parent. He slowly lifted the latch, and found her sitting in her little room mending his clothes. Her eyes were red with weeping, and she was so grieved by his conduct that she hid her face in her hands, and was unable to speak. O, what a return was this for a mother's love and kindness! Ulrich was moved to tears. He fell upon her neck, and begged her forgiveness. She put her arms round him, and forgetting all his unkind looks and reproachful words, pressed him to her bosom. Ulrich promised to love and obey her, and if at any time he felt for a moment disposed to be angry or sullen, he

---

[9] Proverbs 30:17.

remembered the promises and tears of that day, and the words of Father Simon.

    Your affectionate brother,
James

Letter 3

Life is Short

My dear brother,

Life has been compared to the flight of swift ships, and of an eagle hastening to the prey. It is a span, a hand's breadth, a dream. This is the account which the Scriptures give of human life, and if you will consider it, you will see much in it to make you alter your present course of conduct. When a youth looks forward, he almost always thinks of long life. He thinks somewhat in this way: "I am now thirteen, or fifteen, or seventeen years old, (as the case may be). In so many years more I shall be of age. Then I shall be my own master. I will do so and so; I will try such and such schemes; I shall be happy."

Mistaken boy! How different from this does life seem to the old man! *He* looks back, and says to himself: "It was but the other day that I was a boy. I was then full of hope. Life seemed a long and flowery path. I have mistaken it. It is a short journey, through a vale of tears."

From this, we all learn to say with Moses in the ninetieth psalm: "So teach us to number our days, that we may apply our hearts unto wisdom."[10]

Is life short? Then, my dear brother, whatever you have to do in life ought to be done soon. You ought to begin at once. If you were put to a hard task, and an hour-glass were put by you, and you were told, "This sand runs out exactly in an hour, and at the end of the hour I will come to see whether you have done your task;"—how anxious would you be not to lose a moment! Just as anxious should you now be to make a good use of your time. If the whole of life is but a span, then the little portions of it, which we call childhood, youth, middle age, old age, are short indeed. The little portion of youth will soon be over; yet in this very season you are laying a foundation for all the rest of your days. If the young twig grows crooked, the full grown bough will have the same direction fixed. Think of this.

---

[10] Psalm 90:12

Letter 3 – Life is Short

Youth is the gathering time. You must now be busy in laying up useful knowledge for time to come. Youth is the seed-time. If the farmer lets the time of sowing pass by, he will have no harvest in summer, and must starve. If you do not fix in your mind the seeds of truth and wisdom now, you will be ignorant and foolish when you grow to be a man, if you ever do become a man. For you must never forget that multitudes never reach manhood.

Every thing you do, however trifling it may seem, has its bearing upon your future life. You will reap as you sow, and every moment you are sowing some good or some evil. It seems to you no great matter to trifle away an afternoon; but you are thereby getting a habit of idleness—you are losing just so much of life—you are letting just so much sand run down without attending to your assigned task.

The great thing for which you were made is, to please God, and to enjoy his love.[11] Life is short; therefore, do not put off the service of God until tomorrow. If life is so short, you ought to give God the *whole* of it. Surely, you will not rob him of the spring of your days—the very best part of them. He has as much right to this day as to the

---

[11] Note the catechism answer, *"Man's chief end is to glorify God and to enjoy Him forever."*

morrow; he demands your youth as well as your old age. Follow the example of our adorable Redeemer, who said, "I must work the works of him that sent me while it is day; the night cometh when no man can work."[12] This is what few boys think much of; but those who do are wiser and happier when they become older; and none enjoy life so much as those who have early given their affections to Jesus Christ the Lord.

Your affectionate brother,
James

---

[12] John 9:4.

Letter 4

Holidays

My dear brother,

I well remember how much I used to think of holidays when I was a boy. But it pains me to consider how much of this precious time was altogether wasted. But you will say, "Must we study all the time? May we never play?"

Surely, I do not mean this. No one can be a greater friend to recreation than me. I consider it not only harmless, but absolutely necessary. But what I mean is that even in play one should not be foolish or unreasonable. There is such a thing as being profitably employed, at the same time that one is entertained. And there is a certain way of spending holidays so as to get neither profit nor recreation.

MY BROTHER'S KEEPER

Gustavus was a schoolmate of mine, and a more idle lad I never knew. Half his time seemed to be spent in lounging over his books, yawning, stretching, and wishing that the play-hour had come. But how did he use this time of recreation when it came? I think I see him even now. When the Saturday afternoon, or any of the regular holidays came, Gustavus seemed as much at a loss as when he was at his desk in the school-room. He had no plan laid out, no arrangements made for his sports or exercise. Now, I like a boy to have some method even in his play. Gustavus used to saunter along the road on his way homeward, as if he scarcely knew what to do with himself. Then he would put away his books, and come out again. What he was going to do next he could not tell. Sometimes he would lie under the trees, or hang upon the gate, or lounge in the lanes, waiting for some of the other boys to come along. Gustavus was thus more uncomfortable than if he had been at his books. And at the end of a holiday, he used to feel more exhausted and worn out, than his younger brother who had been working in the field. There is no profit in such holidays as these: they encourage idleness and irresolution. You need not be idle even at your plays.

Take another picture of another boy. *Matthew* went to the same school. While he was at his desk he was always employed, and scarcely ever looked away

Letter 4 — Holidays

from his lesson. His whole soul was engaged in it. But when school was out, and books put away, there was not a livelier fellow in the whole school than Matthew: holidays were full of pleasure to him, and full of profit, too. He always had something planned beforehand. Sometimes he had formed a party to climb the neighboring mountains, or to build a fort in the edge of the woods, or to visit some of the villages; sometimes he used to work for hours with the carpenter's tools which his uncle had given him; and thus he received exercise as well as amusement. But what he chiefly loved was to go with his father to walk in the woods, and gather flowers, and learn the names of trees, plants, and minerals.

You will now be able to understand me, when I say, *do not waste your holidays.* One of the most important ways of spending them is in taking active exercise,—a wholesome game at ball, or an hour's ride on a good horse, will fit you for studying so much the better when you return to your lessons. It is a duty for us to take care of our health. Many persons ruin their health in youth; and then it is almost impossible to live either comfortably or usefully.

Visits to your friends may also be paid in your holidays. It is a good sign for boys to be fond of accompanying their mothers and sisters in their visits. Thus they learn good manners, and escape that clownishness which is apt to grow upon students. When I see a boy ready on every knock at the door to sneak out of the room, I naturally conclude that he will never be a well-bred man. And this is more important than you might think at first; for when young men grow up, they need and desire some society. And if they have become so foolishly bashful, or disgracefully awkward, as to shrink from the society of their mothers and sisters, they will be very apt to go out into bad company. Lastly, whatever you do, do it upon principle, do it conscientiously, and you will never regret it.

    Your affectionate brother,
James

Letter 5

Amusements

My dear brother,

You will not be displeased if I devote another letter or two to the subject of recreation and amusement. This is not so trifling a matter as some people might suppose. All young persons are fond of play, and more than this, something of the sort is absolutely necessary. As the proverb says, "the bow must not be always bent,"— and the more diligent a boy is at his books, the more he needs relaxation. This is not only important for the preservation of health, but for preserving the activity and strength of the mind. Constant application, without rest or pastime, wears the mind, and leads to dullness and despondency.

It is very common to leave boys entirely to themselves in the choice of their amusements; but this is not right; for all plays are not alike good, and there are some which are highly injurious and improper.

There are three things which you should have in view in every game or sport: It should be full of *entertainment;* it should be altogether *innocent;* and it should be *of some use* to body or mind. The first requisite, that is entertainment, you will readily seek and find; but boys are not so careful to amuse themselves in a profitable, or even a harmless way. Let me call your attention to some of the amusements which are common.

First of all, I persuade myself that you will never think of playing *cards.* I should wish you never to know even the name of a playing-card. Games of this kind are all games of hazard or chance. They do not benefit the mind, they waste precious time, and, above all, they lead directly to the ruinous vice of gambling. Every play in which dice are used is, in some degree, a game of hazard; and such amusements lead the inexperienced to gambling. *Draughts,* or *checkers,* is a game of skill; but I never could see it to be of much use to the mind, and it certainly affords no advantages to the body. Indeed, all sedentary games of this sort seem unsuitable for youth, because they keep the players within doors, while they might be employed in taking healthful exercise.[13] The game of *chess* is liable also to the last of these objections, although it has been

---

[13] Publisher's Note: Consider the advice of Alexander here as it would relate to such modern amusements as TV, videos and especially video games, all of which consume untold hours in the lives of the young.

Letter 5 — Amusements

approved by many judicious persons. I certainly do not regard it as evil in itself, and it may be true that it encourages thought, and exercises the mind to a certain extent. But its fascinations are such, that most who are fond of it waste many precious hours at the chessboard. It often takes up a great length of time, and those who become experts are frequently tempted to try other games, and so become gamblers at length. Besides, I could never find it as clearly beneficial to the mind as has been pretended. Some of the most wonderful chess-players I have ever seen have been persons of very feeble understanding and limited reasoning powers. In a word, I would recommend to you to abstain from all games which keep you sitting still, and yield no direct improvement.

You are rather too big a boy to engage in the trifling sports of children. Such I consider *marbles*. I am always mortified to see large boys at this pastime. It brings one into bad company, is often connected with a sort of gambling, and at best is somewhat a groveling business, without any pretence of being useful.

There are other recreations which are good or bad, according to the way in which they are used. Such are *wrestling* and *boxing*. These are highly useful to the limbs, affording them exercise and strength. But then care must be taken to avoid all danger, and especially to shun every disposition towards fighting and bullying. I fear it will generally be found that good boxers are apt, to become quarrelsome.

You will, no doubt, expect me to say something about what are called the sports of the field. Among these I include *angling,* or fishing with the hook and line. It is certainly delightful to stroll along pleasant brooks, and to recline on the green, shaded banks, in fine summer weather. And in the pursuit of this sport, it is always pleasing to witness the increase of one's skill, and the corresponding success. Where it is pursued for the sake of obtaining food, it is undoubtedly a reasonable and useful employment. But when boys go a fishing, their sole object is amusement, and their amusement is a cruel one. The baiting with live worms, which writhe upon the barbed hook, and the mangling of the harmless little fish which are caught, are surely bad lessons of humanity for tender youth. Some persons will call these objections weak and womanlike. But where amusements are so abundant, without the necessity of harming any living thing, I cannot see the need of seeking so barbarous enjoyment; and in those respects in which the female sex excels, I am very willing to be considered feminine.

My objections are still greater to *fowling* or gunning for birds, as an amusement for boys. There is

Letter 5 — Amusements

no sport in which they become so enthusiastic, and there are few which are more injurious. Not to speak of the lamentable accidents which are constantly occurring with fire-arms; there is here a greater cruelty than even in angling. If every bird at which you discharged your piece were killed on the spot, there might be less reason for this remark. But how many poor fluttering things are merely wounded, and left to linger for hours or days in mortal anguish. I can never forget the impressions made upon me in my childhood, by the touching lines of Burns,[14] upon seeing a wounded hare limp along his path:

> Inhuman man! shame on thy barbarous art,
> And blasted be thy murder-aiming eye;
> May never pity soothe thee with a sigh;
> Nor ever pleasure glad thy cruel heart.
>
> On live, poor wanderer of the wood and field,
> The bitter little that of life remains;
> No more the thickening brakes and verdant plains
>   To thee shall home or food or pastime yield.
>
> Seek, mangled wretch, some place of wonted rest,
> No more of rest, but now thy dying bed;
> The sheltering rushes whistling o'er thy head;
> The cold earth with thy bloody bosom press'd.
>
> Oft as by winding Nith I musing wait
> The sober eve, or hail the cheerful dawn,
> I'll miss thee sporting o'er the dewy lawn,
> And curse the ruffian's aim, and mourn thy hapless fate.

---

[14] Robert Burns (1759-1796) was one of Scotland's greatest poets.

Whole days are commonly consumed in this sport and there are many young men who become so fond of it as to make it their principal employment. Without enlarging upon the reasons why it is so, I will state it as a fact, which I have long observed, that young men who are devoted to dogs and guns usually become idle and dissipated.

But you will be ready to say, "You are only telling me what past-times I must *not* indulge in; name some which you recommend." This I propose to do in my next communication. In the mean time, let me give you one important rule, which applies to the whole subject: *Let amusement always occupy its proper time.* Its time is when the mind needs refreshment, when it has been jaded by application. Never make a business of play—never spend whole days upon mere recreation. Be moderate in all enjoyments of this kind, and avoid every thing that is frivolous and childish. Remember that we are just as accountable for our relaxation as for any thing else; and we ought, therefore, to be as conscientious in it. Farewell.

Your affectionate brother,
James

Letter 6

Bodily Exercise

My dear brother,

You are not to suppose, from my objections to certain plays and games, that there are no suitable recreations. Indeed, my difficulty in writing to you this morning, is, that there are so many, I scarcely know where to begin, or which to choose. There are amusements which are good for the body, or the mind, or for both. Let us consider a few of these.

Healthful exercise is part of the duty of every day. The divine Maker and Master of these bodies requires that we should take good care of them. Young persons engaged in study are liable to diseases which arise from want of exercise. No day should pass, therefore, without sufficient employment of the limbs and muscles. And those exercises are best which give strength to the body, and at the same time give recreation to the mind. If you amuse yourself without muscular action, you will be puny and weak of limb; and if you take ever so much exercise without delight, you will become dull and melancholy. Try to accomplish both ends at once.

For example, *riding on horseback* is a noble exercise for boys. It is an indispensable part of a manly education. It is one of the best means of preserving health. To manage a spirited horse is quite an attainment for a young man; tending to produce high cheerfulness and courage. In many ways which I cannot stop to name, it may be very useful in your future life. And you will never be an independent rider, unless you become such in your boyhood.

Walking may be used when one cannot ride. But walking takes more time and often fatigues before it has sufficiently excited the circulation, and revived the spirits. Neither can you survey so great a variety of scenes on foot as on horseback. Let me own, however, that the great Dr. Franklin[15] considered walking the very best sort of exercise. It should be pursued for at least two hours every day, by those who study closely. Pedestrian excursions are of great benefit. In this way hundreds of the students at the German universities spend their vacations, sometimes traveling over all Switzerland.

---

[15] Benjamin Franklin (1706-1790) was a famous American Statesman and Inventor.

Letter 6 — Bodily Exercise

Whether you walk or ride, however, you should have a companion; otherwise your thoughts will be apt still to busy themselves with the books you have left. Try to have some object in view, in your walk or ride. Visit a friend—seek out some natural curiosity—make yourself familiar with every hill and valley, every nook and corner, of the whole township and county. In process of time, extend your researches to your own State, and then to other States. Or make collections in mineralogy and botany, that you may be gaining science as well as health. Thus you will become a traveler, and *judicious travel* is the most profitable, as it is certainly the most agreeable of all recreations.

Swimming, rowing, and *skating* are manly sports, and conducive to health when practiced with discretion. The first in particular is essential to a good education; for as you read in Thomson,[16]

> Life is oft preserved
> By the bold swimmer, in the swift illapse
> Of accident disastrous.

I say nothing about trap-ball, cricket, shinny, (sometimes called handy) quoits, and the like,[17] because the only danger is that you already do too much at them. They are all good, when used at proper times, in proper places, and with proper care; but no

---

[16] James Thomson (1700-1748) was a Scottish poet.
[17] Various sports that were popular in that day.

one of them conduces to any immediate benefit, beyond the exercise and amusement. Not so with *manual labor*. This, after all, seems to be the true recreation, especially for wintry days, when we have to keep the house. The Jews used to hold, that every lad, however rich, should he bred to a trade. A little skill in *carpentry* is a grand accomplishment. How often have I regretted that I had not gained it. I might now be independent of the joiner,[18] when I want a new shelf, or when the leg of my table needs to be mended. A *turning lathe* is used by some young friends of mine, with great advantage. Every large school ought to have a good supply of tools, and some one to give lessons to the boys. But even without other tools, you may chop, saw, and split wood, or break up coal, or roll the gravel walks, or ply the wheelbarrow. And when these things are done by boys in concert, nothing can be more entertaining. *Gardening* is so charming a recreation, so innocent, healthful, and profitable, that I might spend a whole letter in writing about it. Take my word for it, if you live to be a man, you will have a peculiar satisfaction in looking at trees or shrubbery which you had put in the earth many years before. And in our climate, where trees for shade are so valuable, you cannot discharge your duty to society, if you do not

---

[18] Joiner – one whose occupation is to construct things by joining pieces of wood together; a mechanic who does the wood-work in the covering and finishing of buildings.

Letter 6 — Bodily Exercise

occasionally plant a linden, or locust, or an elm which may refresh your fellow men when you shall have departed. I am the more earnest about this, because I have to walk daily through a street, upon which the noontide sun pours his beams, much to my discomfort. If I had set out trees twenty years ago, as I might have done, how different would my walks be! Look at the shaded promenade before the State House in Philadelphia, or Temple Street in New Haven, or Bond Street in New York, or the Mall in Boston, and you will feel the force of my advice. The cultivation of valuable fruit trees and plants may be made a source of profit as well as of pleasure.

But I have filled my sheet of paper, and yet am not half done with the subject. Adieu, my dear boy; but remember, in recreation, no less than in labor, to keep a conscience void of offence towards God and towards man.

Your affectionate brother,
James

Letter 7

Early Rising

My dear brother,

In the course of my reading I am always glad to meet with any thing which strikes me as suitable for your instruction. This morning I opened upon a page of Mr. Jay's[19] works, in which he speaks of *early rising*, and his thoughts are so excellent, that I shall make free use of them, and mingle them with my own.

The habit of early rising, if ever formed, is commonly established in childhood or youth. If one has wasted the delightful morning hours of fifteen years in bed, he will not readily learn to deny himself; therefore, I wish you *now* to learn to enjoy,

"The cool, the fragrant, and the silent morn,
To meditation due, and sacred song."

---

[19] William Jay (1769-1853) wrote *Morning Exercises for the Closet* which is the source of this devotional referred to by the author.

Letter 7 — Early Rising

Perhaps you are ready to ask, "How much sleep is necessary?" This cannot be answered in a word. Some need more than others. But Mr. Jay says, "It is questionable whether they require *much* more. Yea, it may be questioned whether they require *any* more, as to length. What they want more of is *better* sleep; and the quality would be improved by lessening the quantity." This remark used to be often made by the celebrated and excellent Dr. Benjamin Rush.[20] Try the experiment of shortening your slumbers; you will have fewer dreams, fewer turnings and tossings but more solid repose, more refreshment.

But you must shorten your rest at the right end; not by sitting up late at night, but by rising early in the morning. Physicians say that one hour's sleep before midnight is worth more than two hours after it. However this may be, one hour of study before breakfast is certainly worth two after supper. The mind is more fresh and cheerful, and the health is less injured. And then, how much more delightful are the early hours! The poet says truly,

"Sweet is the breath of morn, her rising sweet,
With charm of earliest birds."[21]

---

[20] Benjamin Rush (1746-1813) is remembered as a Revolutionary physician, a patient, a reformer, and the "American Hippocrates." He has also been cited as the "Father of American Psychiatry."
[21] John Milton (1608-1674), *Paradise Lost* (bk. IV, l. 641).

In the delightful months of spring, summer, and autumn, you should be up at sunrise. When the vapors begin to disperse, you will observe all nature bedewed with sweetness. Fresh odors breathe from the woods, and fields, and gardens. A thousand birds are singing in the branches. The morning walk among such scenes is as useful to the health as it is pleasing to the taste.

It is time that you should begin to care for your health, and take measures to secure strength for future usefulness. The advantage of early rising, as it regards this, will be apparent in your vigor, your appetite, your nerves, your spirits, and even your complexion. Ask your physician. Is there a medical man on earth that would risk his reputation by a contrary opinion? Dr. Sinclair, in his volumes on health and long life, remarks, that though those who lived to a very great age differed in many things, they all resembled each other here. There was not one who did not rise early.

Whatever business you may ever be engaged in, will be furthered by early rising. What an advantage has a student from this habit in planning and arranging his pursuits for the day! In dispatching what requires haste, whether reading or writing! And in having leisure for any incidental engagement, without putting every thing else into disorder! While another is disposed to cry out, "A little more sleep, and a little

Letter 7 — Early Rising

more slumber,"[22] and who begins at ten what he should have begun at six, is thrown into hurry and confusion; bustles forward to overtake himself; feels himself a drudge all day; and at night is weary, without having accomplished his task. All this is so well known, that those very people who love to lie in bed themselves are very strict in causing their servants to rise in good season; and among all active, business men, a man's reputation suffers from the want of this virtue.

The heathen used to say, *Morning is the friend to the muses.* It surely is a friend to the graces. If it is the best time for study, it is also the best time for devotion. When prayer and praise are neglected in the morning, they are commonly neglected all day; and if you let the world get the start of your soul in the morning, you will seldom overtake it all day. Morning devotion sweetens every succeeding hour, pours a balm on the conscience, gives a pleasant savor to business, locks the door against wicked thoughts, and furnishes matter for pious reflection.

It is better to go from prayer to business than from business to prayer. Intercourse with God prepares for intercourse with our fellow creatures, and for every event, whether pleasing or painful. *Boerhaave*,[23] the

---
[22] Proverbs 24:33.
[23] Herman Boerhaave (1668-1738) was a Dutch Calvinist chemist, physician and professor of medicine who was the first great clinical, or "bedside," teacher.

celebrated physician, rose early in the morning, and through his life his practice was to retire an hour for private prayer and meditation. *Col. Gardiner,* even when in camp, used to spend two hours of the early morning in religious exercises. The great *Judge Hale,* too, rose early, and retired for prayer, and read a portion of God's word, without which, he said, nothing prospered with him all day. *Howard,* the philanthropist,[24] was an early riser. *John Wesley* usually slept five hours; and for many years, he, and all the first Methodist preachers, had a public service at five in the morning. *President Dwight*[25] was in the habit of studying before day for a large portion of his life. And there was in one of our southern States, a laboring man who, by devoting two hours of every morning to study, before he went to his work, became a learned theologian.

If you have already acquired the disgraceful habit of lying in bed late, break it off now, not *gradually,* but *at once.* Do not regard the little unpleasant feelings you may have to endure for a few weeks. Go forth, and inhale the fragrance of the charming spring and autumnal mornings; it will be a cordial to your body and your mind. And in the summer, the season from early dawn until breakfast is the only time you can

---

[24] John Howard (1726-1790), see his story on pp. 108-110 of this book.
[25] Timothy Dwight (1752-1817), theologian was President of Yale.

Letter 7 — Early Rising

enjoy a book, a walk or ride in the open air. Let me give you *Milton's* account of the way in which he used to pass his morning hours. "Those morning haunts," says this great poet, "are where they ought to be—at home; not sleeping or concocting the surfeits of an irregular feast, but up and stirring; in winter, often ere the sound of any bell awake men to labor or devotion; in summer, as oft with the bird that first rouses, or not much tardier, to read good authors, or cause them to be read, till the attention be weary, or memory have its full freight; then with useful and generous labors preserving the body's health and hardiness, to render lightsome, clear, and not lumpish obedience to the mind, to the cause of religion and our country's liberty."

I have written to you more than once, concerning the example of our adorable Savior; and I wish the chief object of these letters may be, to set this blessed example more fully before you. Now, what do you suppose was our Lord's practice? Just imagine to yourself the way in which he spent his morning hours. Can you for an instant suppose that he passed them in slumbers upon his couch? When the hum of business began among the laborers of Judea or of Galilee, and the sun shone warmly on the fields and villages, was the Redeemer asleep? Is it possible for you to think so? No, it is not. On a certain occasion, we read, *"And in the morning, rising up a great while before day, he went out, and departed into a solitary place, and there prayed;"*[26] and yet he had been greatly occupied the whole of the day preceding this. We think little of time, but he never passed an idle hour. The language of the whole of his life was, *"I must work the works of him that sent me, while it is yet day: the night cometh, wherein no man can work."*[27] Yet he was really a man. He took our infirmities, and wearied nature required repose; but he distinguished between what was necessary and what was needless; and it may be also said of his whole life, *"He pleased not himself."*[28]

    Your affectionate brother,
James

---

[26] Mark 1:35.
[27] John 9:4.
[28] Romans 15:3.

Letter 8

The Habit of Diligence

My dear brother,

Not long ago I wrote to you about the importance of forming right habits, and I then said a little upon the subject of diligence. I now wish to write to you more particularly concerning this matter, for this is the time in which you must form the habit of application, if you ever do.

Think how valuable a thing knowledge is. If you take two boys of the same age, one from an Indian tribe, and the other from an intelligent family of Christians, you will observe an amazing difference. I do not mean the difference in their looks, and clothing, and manners, but in their minds. One will be ignorant of almost every thing that is useful. The other will know a thousand things upon a great many subjects. Such is the effect of education. When one of the ancient philosophers was asked what was the use of knowledge, he answered, "Take two men, one educated and the other uneducated, and let them be cast naked upon a foreign coast, and you will see the difference which knowledge makes."

There are many things which we learn without much trouble, by hearing our parents and friends talk about them. But in order to be truly learned, so as to be most useful, we must apply ourselves to study. Many boys are too apt to look upon their lessons as mere tasks. They take no pleasure in learning them, and are glad when they are free from them, in order that they may go and play. This is because they do not consider what a precious thing knowledge is. If they considered this, they would be delighted whenever they have an opportunity to learn any thing.

Let me mention two cases. *Joseph* is a boy of my acquaintance, who has very good talents, and has been sent to school from his infancy. His father has given him the best teachers, and furnished him with all the books that he needs. But still he makes scarcely any improvement. He takes his book, and opens it, and looks at the pages, but seems always ready to fall asleep over it. It is a tiresome business to him. Then he becomes so weary that he frets and grows peevish, looks about the room, plays with his knife and pencil, talks with those who sit next to him, and when he rises

Letter 8 — The Habit of Diligence

to recite his work, is shamefully unprepared. He hates his books, and is sorry when the hour comes for him to go to school. He learns nothing, and is a mere idler. What is the reason? He never thinks of the use of knowledge. He does not consider that this is the very best time for him to get knowledge. Perhaps no one has ever told him how sorry and ashamed he will be when he grows up, and finds that he knows scarcely any thing. Joseph has been so negligent that he has formed a habit of idleness. This habit has grown very strong. His teacher promised him a beautiful book, if he would get one lesson perfectly. Joseph thought he was sure of the prize, and that he could get the lesson in an hour. So he could, easily, if it had not been for this habit of idleness. For two or three minutes he would fix his eye on his book, and seemed to study very hard. But then the old habit would begin to work; he would look off to see what his next neighbor was doing, and before long, he would catch himself playing with the string of his sachet, or cutting notches on his slate-frame. Then he would get back to his book, but in a minute or two he would have forgotten all about it. Joseph got no prize, and I am afraid he will be an ignorant boy as long as he lives.

Benjamin is of the same age, and in the same class, but he is a very different boy. He knows that it gives his dear parents very great pleasure when he is attentive to his tasks. He has often heard of the value of time, and that when it is lost it can never be recovered. And he is sure that the more he studies now, the wiser he will be when he grows up to be a man, if his life should be spared. For these reasons he is very careful to learn as much as he can. He loves his books, and feels pleasure at every new thing which he is taught. He is never idle, but spends the whole of his school-hours in getting his lessons. It is no burden to him to learn, but rather a pleasure; and he is more cheerful and happy when he is at hard study, than the boys around him who are whispering, or playing, or nodding over their books. Benjamin has formed a habit of diligence. It is as natural to him to study when he is at school, as to eat when he is at the table. He knows every lesson perfectly, and gratifies his parents when he goes home, by telling them how many pleasant things he has learned. If Benjamin lives to be a man, he will have a great deal of useful knowledge. For any one who loves to learn will certainly become learned. This habit of application will be likely to stick to him all his life, and he will be learning something good as long as he lives. Now, I wish you to choose between these two boys, and find out which of them you would like to resemble. And whatever habits you *now* form, I think you will always keep.

Letter 8 — The Habit of Diligence

If you have been so unhappy as to neglect this, and have already fallen into any bad habits, I beg that you will try, with all your might, to get rid of them. This is often very hard; for it is more difficult to unlearn what is bad, than to learn what is good. But it must be done; and the sooner the better. Even small things are important, when they become habitual. Plato, the Grecian philosopher, once rebuked a young man very severely for playing with dice. "Why do you rebuke me so severely," said the youth, "for so small a matter?" Plato replied, "It is no small matter to form a habit." While you have your books before you try to think of nothing else. If you find yourself beginning to be weary, rouse your mind by thinking of the value of time, the use of learning, and especially your duty to your God.

Habit will make those things easy which at first seem very hard. By constant practice men become able to do astonishing works. There is a story in ancient books of a man whose strength was so great, that he could carry an ox upon his shoulders. When he was asked how he acquired such power, he said it was by this means: he took the animal when it was a young calf, and lifted it every day, till it grew to this size; and by constant practice his strength grew as the calf grew. You may believe the tale or not, just as you choose; but it is a good illustration of the power of constant practice. It is much the same in learning. In arithmetic, for instance, it is astonishing how some young people will improve by practice. If you were to take a long page in a merchant's ledger, it would take you up to fifteen minutes to add it up; but your father would run his finger up the row of figures, and tell you the sum in less than two minutes. This is because he is practicing it every day. I know many persons who never think of using a slate for any of the common questions in arithmetic; they have the habit of working them all in their head. So also in composition. When you sit down to write a letter, it takes you a long time to think what to put down. You bite your pen, and muse and ponder, and take a great while to fill half a page. But your sister writes on, as fast as her pen will move, and never stops until she has covered the whole sheet. All these things should encourage you to be very much in earnest, and to study diligently, and acquire the habit of using every hour to the best advantage.

There are many young persons who would give all they have in the world for the advantages you possess. They have no books, no friends to teach them, and no money to pay for schooling. If they were in your place, they would go forward with rapid steps. Some poor boys who have labored under all these difficulties, have, nevertheless, become very learned men. In order to excite your mind, I intend, before

Letter 8 — The Habit of Diligence

long, to give you the history of some of these. In the mean-time, my dear brother, *be diligent.* Do every part of your duty *with all your might.* When you *play,* do it heartily, and take as much pleasure in it as you choose; but when you study, do it in good earnest, and do nothing else.

Your affectionate brother,
James

Letter 9

Learning Something Every Hour

My dear brother,

You must not suppose, from what I said in my last letter, that the school is the only place where you can acquire knowledge. I would by no means have you to play all the time that you are not employed at your tasks. There are a great many hours, especially in these long winter evenings, in which you may be filling your mind with something useful. For this purpose you should always have some instructive book at hand. Your parents have many such books, and are always glad to give you the use of them. It makes me sorry to see that you read so much in mere story books. Some of these, indeed, are useful, and they are liked by all young people; but most of them are foolish, if not injurious. Boys often become so fond of this sort of reading that they never look into any thing but tales

Letter 9 — *Learn Something Every Hour*

and novels. And in this way they weaken their minds, and lose all the advantage they might gain from books of instruction. Now, if you did but think of it, you would find out that there are works which are highly entertaining, at the same time that they are profitable. I mean books of history, voyages and travels, biography, natural history, and philosophical experiments. If you were once to taste the pleasantness of these, you would soon throw away your story books, which are mostly fit for the nursery.

But you cannot be always reading, and it is by no means necessary. There are many other ways of getting useful knowledge. The greater part of what you already know, you have learned from hearing your father and mother talking. If all they have told you should be written down, it would fill a multitude of volumes. And you remember this much better than if you had read it in a book. You ought, therefore, to learn something every day from your parents. They are always willing to teach you; and whenever you have any difficulty you should get them to explain it. There are a thousand things which they would be delighted to tell you and which you would be glad to learn. Whenever you are sitting with them, try to get them to instruct you. You may do the same thing with all your friends. If you are only modest and respectful, they will not consider you too inquisitive. All sensible people are gratified when they see that boys are desirous to learn. Make it a rule to learn something from everybody; for there is no one, high or low, who has not some knowledge which might do you good. For instance, you have friends in the school who come from different parts of the country. You may gain much information from them, by inquiring concerning the places where they live, and getting them to describe to you every thing that is remarkable in their own neighborhoods. Even the tradesmen and mechanics can instruct you in many little matters relating to their own employments. It is a great advantage for a man to know something about every different trade and mechanic art, and you cannot learn this from books so well as from going into the workshops, and asking questions of the people who are at work. When they see that you really wish to be informed, they will he glad to answer all your inquiries. I should like you to know all the particulars about every kind of trade and manufacture.

And then, when you go into the country, it will make your excursions much more pleasant if you will take pains to learn from farmers every thing about the cultivation of the earth. You must be sure to find out as much as you can about the different operations of agriculture; sowing, reaping, and the like; and about the productions of the land, the raising of cattle and

Letter 9 — Learn Something Every Hour

sheep, and the ways of improving the soil. You will find that many husbandmen, who have not read as much as yourself, have a great treasure of knowledge and wisdom. Sometimes you will fall into the company of those who have traveled in foreign countries. This will give you a fine opportunity to learn from them all you wish to know about the parts of the world which they have visited. And if you travel about in your holidays, you must keep your eyes open to every thing that is remarkable, and learn all about the places through which you pass. In old times this was the principal way of acquiring knowledge. Instead of going to colleges and universities, the ancient Greeks used to travel for years together in Asia and Egypt, and other lands. This is the method which was pursued by Lycurgus, and Pythagoras, and Plato,[29] and others of whom your histories tell you. When you go to a strange place, you must endeavor to find out, whatever is curious, and to make inquiries of all your friends.

There are a great many common things which we see every day, that are very curious. Many boys carry watches for months and years without knowing at all what it is that makes them go. *Charles Harvey* had a watch given to him the day he was fifteen years old. He was much pleased with the present, but could not

---

[29] Lycurgus (c. 396-325, BC), Pythagoras (c. 582-500, BC), and Plato (c. 428-347 BC).

feel satisfied until he went to the watchmaker, and got him to explain the inside of it. The watchmaker took the watch to pieces, and showed him all the works. He showed him the *steel spring* wound up in a coil, and let him see how it was constantly trying to unwind itself and get loose. Then he showed him the *barrel* to which the end of the spring is fastened, and how the working of the spring makes the barrel move round and round. He pointed out the *chain* which goes from the barrel to the *great wheel* and *fusee*,[30] and told him how one wheel moved another, till the *hands* were made to go round. But you cannot understand this by writing. If you ask your father, he will explain all these works to you in a few minutes.

Some boys are so careless that they make no inquiries, and never learn any thing of value. I knew a boy who used to go to a mill every few days, but who never had the curiosity to ask how it was that the water falling on the great wheel could make the mill-stone turn round: and lads will often own guns without ever finding out how the lock is formed, or how the trigger moves the other works, or how the gunpowder or the shot is made. I hope it will not be so with you, but that whenever you see any machine, you will not rest until you know all about it. When you are next on board of

---

[30] An ingenious device which compensates for the declining force of a mainspring as it unwinds by automatically adjusting the gearing between the spring and the *train* as it runs.

Letter 9 — Learn Something Every Hour

a steamboat, get someone to explain to you how the steam works. Inquire about the boiler, and the condenser, and the piston, and the valves. Find out the way in which the pump in the yard raises the water, and what it is that makes the mercury rise and fall in the thermometer.

The great thing is to be always inquiring. *Ask and you will learn.* Learn something every hour. Remember the little story of *Eyes and no Eyes,* and read *Travels about Home.*[31] Whenever you take a walk, you may be learning something. You ought to be able to tell the name of every kind of tree in the woods, either by the bark and leaves, or by the shape, and the way they look at a distance. You may easily find out the names of the principal plants and flowers which grow in the fields. It will be a shame if you grow up without knowing how to tell one bird from another, by their shape, their plumage, their song, or their manner of flying. When you come to look more sharply, you will discover a great many curious differences in the mosses and the ragged lichens which grow on the fences and stones, and look like mould. This is the way to become a philosopher. A philosopher is a lover of wisdom. The reason why some men become philosophers is that they are always inquiring and learning something every hour. It was thus that Dr.

---

[31] These works were published by the American Sunday-school Union.

Franklin became so celebrated, and discovered the nature of thunder and lightning, which no one knew before. I have read also of poor shepherd's boys who have become great philosophers in the same way.

If you are only determined to be learning something all the time, there is no doubt that you will be constantly improving. When your friends see this they will help you, and be glad to instruct you. They will put you in the way of making experiments for yourself, and will furnish you with books and instruments. Thus your very amusements will be full of profit. I am sure that you would find far more entertainment in trying experiments with a little electrical machine than in playing at ball or marbles. And at the same time you would be learning an important science. You might spend an hour or two in a printing office, learning the way in which books are made, and be much more amused than by running about the playground.

So you see that even when you are not in school you may be constantly improving your mind. You cannot open your eyes anywhere without beholding something to inquire about; and the more inquiries you make, the more you will know. This makes one great difference between people; some are anxious to learn, while others do not care whether they learn or not. Be awake, my dear brother, and remember that time is short, and that you must give an account of the way in

Letter 9 — Learn Something Every Hour

which you spend every moment. The greater your knowledge is, the more useful you may be to your fellow creatures.

Your affectionate brother,
James

Letter 10

Three Self-taught Scotch Lads

My dear brother,

You have good teachers and parents who delight in giving you all the books and all the instructions which you need. For these favors you ought to be thankful to your heavenly Father; and this should make you more diligent than you have ever been before. I wish to give you some account, at this time, of the way in which certain young persons, without your advantages, became truly learned. I hope that when you see how much progress they made, with every thing against them, you will be encouraged to greater perseverance and improvement of your time.

Did you ever hear of a man named *Edmund Stone?* He was born about a hundred and thirty years ago, in Scotland.[32] Edmund's father was gardener to

---

[32] Edmund Stone (1700-1768).

Letter 10 — Three Self-taught Scotch Lads

the Duke of Argyle. This nobleman one day found on the grass a volume of a book called *Newton's Principia,* in Latin, and when he made inquiries, learned that it belonged to young Edmund. He was much astonished to find that his gardener's son could read Latin, or understand mathematics. He said to him, "But how came you by the knowledge of all these things?" "A servant," said the youth, who was then in his eighteenth year, "taught me to read ten years ago. Does one need to know any thing more than the twenty-four letters in order to learn every thing else that one wishes?" The duke was still more surprised; he sat down upon a bank, and received from Edmund the following account:

"I first learned to read," said he, "when the masons were at work upon your house. I approached them one day, and observed that the architect used a rule and compass, and that he made calculations. I inquired what might be the meaning and use of these things, and I was informed that there was a science called arithmetic, and I learned it. I was told there was another science called geometry; I bought the necessary books, and I learned geometry. By reading, I found that there were good books in these two sciences in Latin; I bought a dictionary, and I learned Latin. I understood, also, that there were good books of the same kind in French; I bought a dictionary, and I

MY BROTHER'S KEEPER

learned French. And this, my lord, is what I have done; it seems to me that we may learn every thing when we know the twenty-four letters of the alphabet." This man afterwards became well known as an author, and published a number of mathematical works.

I will now give you some account of another young Scotchman who was still more extraordinary. I mean the astronomer *James Ferguson*.[33] He was born in 1710, in Banffshire. His father was a poor but pious day-laborer. James, by hearing his elder brothers taught, learned to read before his father supposed that he knew the letters. When he was seven or eight years old, he began to pay attention to mechanical contrivances, and actually discovered the principles of the lever, and of the wheel and axle. He was employed as a shepherd, and while his flock was feeding around him, he used to spend his time in making little mills, spinning-wheels, and the like. At night he used to busy himself in looking at the stars. He afterwards was employed by a farmer named Glashan, who was very kind to him. After his day's work, James used to go at night to the fields, with a blanket around him, and a lighted candle, and lie down on his back to examine the stars. "I used," says he, "to stretch a thread with small beads upon it, at arm's length, between my eye and the stars; sliding the beads upon it, till they hid

---

[33] James Ferguson (1710-1776).

such and such stars from my eye, in order to take their apparent distances from one another; and then laying the thread down on a paper, I marked the stars thereon by the beads." Mr. Gilchrist, the minister, showed him how to draw maps, and gave him compasses, rules, &e. In his twentieth year he went to live in the house of a Mr. Grant, whose butler taught him how to make dials, and also instructed him in arithmetic. After his return to his father's house, he procured a book of geography, and made a globe of wood, which he covered with paper, and drew a map of the world on it. This he did before he had ever seen an artificial globe. Next he was employed by a miller, and here he lived so poorly, that often his only fare was a little oatmeal and water. After being some time in the service of a physician, he returned home again, in ill-health. Here he made a wooden clock, and then a wooden watch, without the least assistance or instruction. From this he went on and made some dials. Afterwards he became a painter, but still gave most of his time to philosophy; so that in the end he was a distinguished author, and a member of the Royal Society.

Such accounts as these ought to make you ashamed to be idle. If a gardener and a shepherd's boy, in the midst of hard work, could learn so much without any teachers, how much might you acquire, who have nothing to do but to learn, and have the continual assistance of friends and teachers!

But there is still another Scotchman, whom shall introduce to your acquaintance, namely, the late *Dr. Alexander Murray.*[34] *He was* born in the shire of Kirkcudbright, in 1775, and was the son of a shepherd. He learned to write and read at once, for his father used to draw the letters for him on the board of an old wool-card, with a bit of burnt stick. Much of his time was passed in writing with coals, and he became wonderfully familiar with the Scriptures. His mother's brother, when he was about nine years old, took him to New Galloway, to school, where he lost his health. For a number of years, his only reading was the Bible, and such penny ballads as are hawked about the streets. In 1787, he read Josephus, and Salmon's geography he then undertook to teach the children of two farmers, and for a winter's work received sixteen shillings. He then went to school again, and learned arithmetic and bookkeeping.

The reading of Salmon's geography had led him to think much about foreign countries, and their languages. "I had," says he, "in 1787 and 1788, often admired and mused on the specimens of the Lord's prayer in every language, found in Salmon's grammar. I had read in the Magazine and Spectator that Homer,

---

[34] Alexander Murray (1775-1813).

Letter 10 — Three Self-taught Scotch Lads

Virgil, Milton, Shakespeare, and Newton were the greatest of mankind. I had been early informed that Hebrew was the first language, by some good religious people. In 1789 an old woman showed me her psalm book, which was printed with a large type, had notes on each page, and likewise what I discovered to be the Hebrew alphabet, marked letter after letter in the 119th Psalm. I took a copy of these letters by printing them off in my old way, and kept them." He undertook to teach himself French, and from this he went to the Latin grammar, of which he borrowed a copy from a boy. And this extraordinary child, with hardly any assistance, was pursuing at one time the study of Latin, French, Greek, and Hebrew. But I cannot go on to mention all the languages he learned. There was probably no man living who knew so many, and in all of these he was self-taught. He wrote some of the most learned works which have ever appeared, and died at the early age of thirty-eight. It was his thirst for knowledge and his constant application which made him learned; and this shows the truth of what I before told you,—that he who is really desirous of acquiring information will always succeed.

I might mention other instances. William Gifford,[35] the late learned editor of the Quarterly Review, was first a sailor-boy on a coal vessel, and

---

[35] William Gifford (1756-1826).

then a shoemaker. He used to learn mathematics while he was making shoes, and having no pen or paper, he beat out pieces of leather as smooth as possible, and wrought his problems on them with a blunted awl. In the same way he used to write verses. He afterwards became one of the most celebrated scholars. And there are many other such cases which I can point out for your perusal in various books. But I must now conclude, heartily wishing that you may profit by whatever is good in every example.

    Your affectionate brother,

James

Letter 11

Formation of Habits

My dear brother,

Some of the subjects upon which I intend to address you, will perhaps seem small. Nothing is small, however, or unimportant, which concerns the forming of your habits. You are now forming a character for life, and, as I have intimated in a former letter, ten years hence it will be too late to amend what is done amiss now.

Near the place where I write, a number of men are busied in building a large house. They are carrying up thick walls of solid stone. Now I observe that they are very careful in laying these stones. They are constantly measuring with the rule and the plummet, to make every part exactly as it should be. And they have reason for this, because, if, six months hence, they should find out that their wall was not perpendicular, or their foundation not strong, they could do nothing to remedy it, but to take down their work and do it over again. So it is with you. Every habit you form is one stone laid in your character. At this early age you may correct bad habits, but it will be all but impossible when you shall have become a man. Besides, the character of a youth is fixed, as to great matters, much sooner than many suppose. Not long ago, I came to a place in which I had spent many of my youthful days, and saw several of my playmates. They are now men and women, and some of them have children as old as I was when we all went to school together. Other changes have taken place, but in almost every one I see the same general character.

Let me give you an instance. There is John Smith, who was the most diligent boy in the school. He is still diligent, and has gained so much knowledge that he is thought to be the wisest lawyer in the State. There is Samuel Johnson, who was idle, sleepy, careless, fond of his bed, and fond of eating. He is still the same sluggish creature; he still rises several hours after the sun; he eats, and drinks, and slumbers. His little property is gone; his coat is out at the elbows; he has lately been released from imprisonment, and will be *Lazy Sam* (I fear) as long as he lives.

Religion, I know, works great and happy changes in some, even late in life. But what I desire for you is, that religion may work this change early in life or

Letter 11 — Formation of Habits

rather that the grace of God may so mould your character *now,* that in these particulars there may be no need of a change so radical. For it is better to lay the foundation right at the beginning, than to tear down the whole walls to put right what is found to be wrong. That is, it is better for a boy to form right habits, from the fear of God, in his boyhood, than to live in wrong habits twenty years, and then try to change them when it is too late. I know some pious persons who are mourning every day over the bad habits of their childhood. Thus they know it is a sin to be slothful, yet they find it too late to acquire diligence, and they lounge all day over newspapers, or trifling conversation, when they might be doing something to benefit their own souls or those of their neighbors.

The proverb of the ancients is good, *Do what is right, however unpleasant, and custom will make it delightful. You* know a little boy, who lives near you, who makes it a rule to walk four miles before breakfast every morning. When he began this it was very irksome, and he was often tempted to give it up; but his father told him that "custom would make it delightful," and he persevered. This became true; he would not now miss his morning walk on any account. I have no doubt he will retain the habit through life, and it will probably keep him a robust, healthy man for many years. Those little things which seem hard to you, in your studies, are of the same kind. Do not give way, like a coward, to every difficulty. It is like diving into the river, which you used to do with me; the first dash only is disagreeable. Make it a rule to conquer difficulties. In this respect be a man at once. In your Latin, your arithmetic, or your exercises, *be brave*. Form a habit of not leaving any thing *half-done*. In the long run it is the easiest way to master every thing before you leave it. Some boys, for instance, never learn the Greek verb perfectly. This they might do in a few days. But they prefer skimming over the lesson, and leave the master to help them out. Now, just look at what follows; every day, as long as they learn Greek, they feel their need of this knowledge. Every day they are mortified, if not disgraced or punished. Yet the *habit of negligence* sticks by them. It creeps into other things. For the very same reasons, they are negligent in composition, in mathematics, and in oratory. They fix the habit for life, and for life are negligent fellows.

Remember, my dear brother, that it is not what you actually learn that is solely important. By learning this or that, you not only treasure up such and such things in your memory, but you discipline your mind. That is, you form *habits* of mind. When a person's mind is tutored into good habits, he is said to have a disciplined mind. One may learn a great many things,

Letter 11 — Formation of Habits

and yet have an undisciplined mind, because he learned them carelessly, hastily, or in the wrong order. Just as the poor beggar, who used to come to our door, knew more poetry than all of us put together, while he was so far from being wise that he could not put two ideas together in the way of reasoning. You are young, and cannot choose for yourself what is best. But your teachers select those studies which will tend to give your mind proper habits. Pay all possible attention to these studies. Be perfect in them. Every *hour now* is worth more to you than a *day* is to me. Every day is confirming you in some habit, either good or bad. And if you are not careful to aim at those which are good, you will most assuredly fall into such as are bad. You cannot be too much in earnest then; attend to every thing which your teacher advises. Several things are apt to be neglected by boys which they find very important when they come to be men. Your time of rising, your attention to personal neatness, your punctuality at school, your bodily exercise, your pronunciation and manners, your temperance and self-denial, your accuracy in study, all these things are contributing to make you (if your life should be spared) a useful, agreeable, wise and happy man, or a disgusting, ignorant, and discontented booby.

Your affectionate brother,

James

Letter 12

Dangers of Evil Companions

My dear brother,

From your earliest infancy you have been taught to avoid bad companions and I hope you see the importance of this more and more. Our manners, our habits, and our ways of thinking are gathered very much from the persons with whom we associate. If you are pleased with the society of idle, irreligious, or profane boys, it is a sure sign that you are already corrupted. And the longer you continue in their company the more you will be injured.

In every school there are some lads who are seducers and corrupters of the rest. They are not always rude or insolent, nor so openly wicked as to shock you at the first acquaintance. Often they are young persons of good manners and gentle behavior; but under this cloak, they are false, malignant, or licentious. When you first become acquainted with them,

Letter 12 — Dangers of Evil Companions

you are charmed by their pleasant deportment; and it is not for a good while that you find out their real character.

There is a saying of a Latin poet which is very true, "No one ever became profligate all at once." The first steps are very slight. The progress is almost imperceptible. When a boy who has been piously educated first comes among ungodly companions, he is shocked with their wickedness. He trembles when he hears them profane the name of God, and retreats from their presence. Their immodest conversation causes him to blush. When they tell willful falsehoods, he is frightened at their daring. After having been some time in their company, this alarm and horror give way. He still dislikes their wicked words and actions, but his ear becomes familiar to the unholy sounds, and he grows used to their impieties. Perhaps a boyish curiosity leads him to mingle in their circle, and listen to their tales. By degrees he is indifferent to what at first so much startled him. *"Evil communications corrupt good manners,"*[36] and he grows more and more like his company. Unless restrained by divine grace, he becomes worse every day. Beginning with foolish exclamations and minced oaths, he at length desires to appear manly and spirited, and ventures upon some profane expression. At his first oath, it is

---

[36] 1 Corinthians 15:33.

likely he turns pale or feels an inward shuddering. But by degrees this goes off. He is shamed out of his early principles, and tries to let his companions see that he is as fearless as themselves. So he proceeds, (if not hindered) until he becomes a complete profligate.

Alas! this is the course of many a young man over whom the tears of piety have been shed. Many a youth has thus gone on, till he has broken a tender mother's heart, and brought down her "gray hairs with sorrow to the grave."[37] Evil company is one of the chief things which corrupt youth. Without bad companions, they would not learn to swear, to curse, or to use indelicate language; without bad companions, they would not be tempted to taste intoxicating drinks, to play at games of hazard, or to practice dishonesty. It is likely that Satan tempts quite as much by wicked persons (who are his tools) as he does directly by his own suggestions to our hearts.

As no one can touch pitch[38] without being defiled, so no young person can be much with wicked playmates without being corrupted. Do not be deceived about this. We all think a great deal of our own resolution, and perhaps you will flatter yourself that you are not to be influenced by bad companions. "Let him that thinketh he standeth take heed lest he

---

[37] Genesis 42:38; 44:29,31.
[38] Any of various thick, dark, sticky substances obtained from the distillation residue of coal tar, wood tar or petroleum.

Letter 12 — Dangers of Evil Companions

fall."[39] The only safety is in flight. You cannot sincerely pray, "Lead us not into temptation,"[40] if you rush into bad company, which is one of the very worst of all temptations. It may be the duty of some persons to go among the wicked, to do them good; just as it may be the duty of some persons to go into a fire, to put it out. But it would be the height of presumptuous folly to walk through the raging flames without necessity; and it is just as presumptuous and as foolish to frequent the society of the wicked.

One of the principal disadvantages of irreligious company is that it prevents or destroys serious impressions on the heart. As soon as wicked youth perceive that one of their number is thinking about religion, they all turn upon him in ridicule. And in too many cases they are successful. The poor deluded coward is more afraid of their scorn than of the wrath of God. He is ashamed to let it be known that he prays or reads the Bible. Thousands and thousands have thus been drawn away from the door of life by the taunts of scoffers. Now, my dear brother, as you value your immortal soul, beware of this. Never be ashamed of Christ. And to avoid this temptation, avoid all wicked companions. Consider carefully who your intimate associates are. If there is among them a single boy who

---

[39] 1 Corinthians 10:12.
[40] Matthew 6:13.

is idle, profane, lewd, deceitful, false, or quarrelsome, *shun that boy.* Break off all acquaintance with him at once. Have as little to say to him and to do with him as possible. You need not offend him, but you must assuredly avoid him. The psalmist describes the good man as one who "walketh not in the counsel of the ungodly, nor standeth in the way of sinners, nor sitteth in the seat of the scornful."[41] Solomon says, "My son, if sinners entice thee, consent thou not: my son, walk not thou in the way with them, refrain thy foot from their path."[42] Read also the following passages: "Enter not into the path of the wicked, and go not in the way of evil men; *avoid it, pass not by it, turn from it, and pass away.*" "Forsake the foolish, and live, and go in the way of understanding." "He that walketh with the wise shall be wise; but a companion of fools shall be destroyed."[43]

By acting in the way which I recommend, it is possible that you may displease some of your schoolmates; but it is better to displease them than to offend God. And in the end, it is very likely that even they will see that your way of life is better than theirs. Remember, that the path of youth is beset with dangers, and ask help of God, and instruction from his

---

[41] Psalm 1:1.
[42] Proverbs 1:10.
[43] Proverbs 4:2; 9:6; 13:20.

Letter 12 — Dangers of Evil Companions

word. "How shall a young man cleanse his way? By taking heed thereto according to thy word."[44] Farewell.

Your affectionate brother,

James

---

[44] Psalm 119:9.

Letter 13

Friendships

My dear brother,

"Tell me your company," says an ancient proverb, *"and I will tell you what you are."* This is a text on which I have several times enlarged in my previous letters. It is a sentiment which you should constantly remember, for it will make your friendships safe and delightful, and will also preserve you from many of the misfortunes into which unwary youth are prone to fall.

But after you have made choice of your acquaintances, after you have discouraged the familiarities of wicked youth, and formed a little circle of proper companions, it is right that you should pay special attention to another point of duty. It is the regulation of your conduct towards those with whom you are intimate. In this particular, boys are always unguarded; every one is liable to err on one side or the other. I hope, therefore, that a few brief directions may

Letter 13 — Friendships

not be thrown away upon you, but will be taken up with all diligence.

Be cautious and slow in choosing your friends. This is what you have already learned, and it is merely introductory to the rules and counsels which follow.

When you have acquired a good friend, be firm and constant in your attachment. It is very disgraceful to abandon a friend without cause. None are so ready to sin in this way as those rash youth who are too hasty in becoming intimate with every new acquaintance. The natural consequence is, that after a few days or weeks, they begin to perceive faults which they had not previously allowed themselves time to discern. They then become disgusted, grow cool in their affection, and are forced to look around them for some new associate. Such was the manner of *Julius*. Whenever a new student arrived, Julius was the first to take him by the hand. And this was not a mere pretence, for he felt the friendship he professed. But he did not take time to study the character of his playmates, and therefore it was only two or three days before he found out some foible in the newcomer, and cast him off as speedily as he had at first embraced him. Then he attached himself to another, and another; and so he went on, until he had, at some time or other, been familiar with the whole school, and had abandoned them all in turn. Julius changed his friends almost as often as his clothes. Such a young man is incapable of true friendship; and his reigning fault is soon discovered by every one. Julius is despised as a fickle and changeable fellow.

Beware of trusting too much to the professions of your companions. I would not have you surly, morose, or suspicious; but all is not gold that glitters. The human heart is deceitful, and those who really love you today may be altered tomorrow. When you have tried a friend, and found him faithful, you may safely confide to him even your private thoughts; but take care that you are not deceived. Especially avoid the practice of telling secrets, particularly the secrets of other people, to your young acquaintances. It is a general rule, which it will be safe for you to observe, never to confide a secret to any one, unless you want either advice or assistance. For, if you cannot keep your own counsel, how can you expect others to keep it for you? Whenever, therefore, you meet with a person who is frequently taking you aside, to whisper something into your ear, *"in confidence,"* you may be sure he is an unsafe companion. Tell no secrets of your own to such a one; and listen to as few of his as possible.

Cherish a warm attachment to your friends when they are in any trouble. "A friend in need is a friend indeed." And Solomon says: "He that is a friend must

Letter 13 — Friendships

show himself friendly."[45] To forsake a companion in the time when he most needs your assistance is base, it is inhuman. The very heathen may teach us a good lesson on this subject. "The name of friendship," says Ovid,[46] "touches the hearts of the very barbarians." Cicero[47] wrote a whole book on the subject of friendship, and it is full of excellent sentiments. You have perhaps read the beautiful anecdote of *Damon and Pythias;* it is related by Valerius Maximus.[48] Damon was condemned to death by Dionysius[49] the tyrant. He obtained leave, however, to go home and settle his affairs, promising to return to the place of execution at a certain hour. And his friend Pythias surrendered himself to the tyrant, and agreed that if Damon was not there at the time, he would himself suffer the punishment in his place. Dionysius naturally concluded that Pythias was a fool, and that Damon would be glad of such an opportunity to escape. But, behold! when the hour arrived, to the astonishment of all, Damon appeared punctually at the place, and declared that he was ready to die. The cruel king was touched by this ardent friendship; he forgave the

---

[45] Proverbs 18:24.
[46] Ovid (43 BC – AD 18) was a famous Roman poet.
[47] Marcus Tullius Cicero (106-43 BC) was Rome's greatest orator and writer of verse, letters and works of philosophy.
[48] Valerius Maximus was a Latin writer, author of a collection of historical anecdotes, flourished in the reign of Tiberius.
[49] A wicked Roman emperor hundreds of years before Christ.

offender, and begged that he might be numbered among their friends.

This reminds me also of a severe saying of the cynic Diogenes.[50] When he was asked how Dionysius treated his friends, he replied, "Just as one treats earthen vessels; when they are full, he empties them; when they are empty, he throws them aside."

Be forbearing towards the faults of a friend. True, you must not love or copy his faults; indeed, it is an important part of friendship to reprove and correct them. But do not abandon an acquaintance for a few faults, or even for a great one, if he has been truly faithful, and if you are not endangered by his example.

Cherish a mild and benevolent temper in all your intercourse. An irritable young man can scarcely be a good companion; and the ill-humor is contagious. The wisest of kings teaches us this lesson: "Make no friendship with an angry man; and with a furious man thou shalt not go; lest thou learn his ways, and get a snare to thy soul."[51]

Never do a wrong thing for the sake of friendship. If you seriously observe this rule, it will keep you from a thousand mischiefs. When *Pericles*[52] was asked by an intimate acquaintance to bear false witness for

---
[50] A Greek philosopher who, along with Antisthenes is considered the founder of The Cynic Philosophy.
[51] Proverbs 22:24.
[52] Pericles, "The Olympian" (495-429 BC).

Letter 13 — Friendships

him, that great man answered, "I am your friend only to the altars," meaning, that he would go as far to help him as religion would allow.

Try to make salutary impressions on the minds of your friends. Many thousands have been converted by means of friendly admonition. If our acquaintances were sick, we would try to heal them; how much more should we try to save their souls! A single word of affectionate advice sometimes does more good than many sermons. And when a youth professes to serve God, he ought to be neither ashamed nor afraid to open his lips in behalf of his Master's cause.

I trust these few directions (which I might multiply a hundred-fold) will be carefully read by you, and faithfully put into practice.

Your affectionate brother,

James

Letter 14

Good Example

My dear brother,

When I wrote to you about the dangers of evil companions, I did not wish you to suppose that you must avoid all society. This would be very wrong, and would make you mopish and sullen. I desire you to frequent the company of all such young friends as can do you good; and I hope there are some whose example you would do well to follow. When you find such a one, who is diligent, kind, respectful, and serious, you will act wisely to be as much as possible with him, and to follow in his steps.

It is very true, as is often said, that *example speaks louder than words*. We often think that certain things are impossible until we see them done by others, and then we begin to attempt them ourselves. There is something in our nature which leads us to imitate the example of those around us. It is thus that

Letter 14 — Good Example

all the boys in a school will have the same sports and pastimes; one learns from another, until they all go in the same path. Now you should take care to follow none but good examples; and here you will have to be very cautious, for our evil hearts lead us more naturally to what is evil than to what is virtuous. There is nothing mean or low in copying the good example of your friends. It is in this way that some of the best and greatest men have become what they are.

I would recommend to you to read the lives of persons who have been remarkable for their knowledge or their goodness. When these memoirs are well written, it is almost as if we were acquainted with the living persons, seeing them act and hearing them speak. There is no kind of reading which is more entertaining than biography, and there is none which is more instructive. In this way you may be constantly setting before your mind the brightest examples, and this will stir you up to be more active in trying to improve. I have never found any books which made me more anxious to excel, than good biographical sketches. When you read of a person who has raised himself from ignorance and obscurity to learning and honor, by his own endeavors, a laudable emulation will lead you to imitate his excellence. Thus the Life of Dr. Franklin has caused many a young mechanic to store his mind with knowledge.

But the best of all biographies are those which are contained in the Holy Scriptures. Have you ever taken notice how much of the Bible is filled with the memoirs of good men? The reason of this no doubt is, that example is so much more powerful than precept. The four gospels contain the memoirs of our Lord Jesus Christ. And they are so beautifully simple, so exact, and so touching, that we seem to see the blessed Redeemer, holy and benevolent, going about doing good, healing the sick, cleansing the lepers, raising the dead. We seem to hear him speaking as never man spoke, and the influence of his example is most powerful upon the mind of the serious reader. My dear brother, read these lovely histories every day. Try to frame in your mind all the circumstances of the scenes there described. Endeavor to feel that it is Christ himself who is speaking to you, and let his words sink into your heart. Find out how he acted under all different circumstances, and then copy his example. How did he treat his parents? (cf. Luke 2:48,51). How did he feel towards the afflicted? How did he act when he was reviled and persecuted? What was his manner as to prayer and devotion? Every hour of the day be careful to ask yourself how the Lord Jesus would have acted under similar circumstances.

It is an advantage for young people to keep company with those who are older and wiser; but there

Letter 14 — Good Example

are few youth who have any taste for this kind of society. They are too apt to think that elderly persons are sour and gloomy. And sometimes, it cannot be denied that those who are advanced in years do not take pains to gratify the inquiries of the young and to do them good. When, however, you find any aged man who loves to give instruction to the young, and whose example is beautiful and pure, try to be as much with him as possible. I have known such a one.

Benevolus is a man of sixty years. His hair is white with age, and he is too feeble to leave the house. But he is happy, because he has faith in Christ, and enjoys the love of God shed abroad in his heart. There is nothing peevish or morose about him, and he welcomes the visits of all his young relatives and friends. He delights in teaching them what is good, and in giving them the history of his early days. And all who come into his presence see the excellence of true religion, and the advantage of having a mind stored with useful knowledge.

I have said so much about *following* good examples, that it will be less needful for me to explain the importance of your *setting* a good example to others. No one of us is allowed to live for himself alone, but we must all endeavor to do good to others. We are commanded to let our light shine before men. You must not suppose that, because you are so young, nobody will follow your example. If you do what is wrong, others of your companions will be encouraged to do the same; and if you do what is right, you may be a blessing to all around you. One boy in a school will often be of service to all the rest, just in this way. I will give you an instance of such a case, and take notice that I sometimes invent names, because I have reasons for not mentioning the individuals.

Tyro was a young lad of about fourteen. He was sent to a school where most of the boys were very idle. They cared but little about the improvement of their minds, and were constantly engaged in sports and mischief. Tyro tried to set them a better example. He got every lesson perfectly, and he assisted others in their tasks. He made it his amusement to read more than was assigned for his lesson, and he induced some of the idle fellows to become diligent. He put them in the way of attempting new studies, and of writing compositions. He persuaded them to form a little society for mutual improvement, and had many little plans of this kind, for their benefit. The consequence was that I never saw a school of the same extent, in which there were so many fine scholars. And I am sure that Tyro was more influential in this than even the teacher himself. Think of this example.

You cannot go through life without having some influence upon others. This influence is either for good

Letter 14 — Good Example

or for evil. You may be either a blessing or a curse. Pray and strive that your example may do good to all around you. Endeavor to lead others in the right way, especially the way of religion. You cannot begin this too soon, and in future life, it will be very pleasing for you to look back and see that you had early begun to be useful to your fellow creatures. Ask assistance from above, that you may be enabled to live in this way. And remember that many eyes are fixed upon you, to see how you will act, and that the happiness of your friends, and especially of your affectionate parents, depends greatly upon your conduct.

Your affectionate brother,

James

Letter 15

Truth and Falsehood

My dear brother,

Few names are considered more disgraceful than that of a *liar*. This is justly so; for the vice is odious, injurious to society, and offensive to God. Truth is the chief bond between man and man in society. If every one spoke without regard to truth, our reputation, property, and lives would be in jeopardy every moment. We should never know when to believe a neighbor; or by believing a falsehood, we might be led into the greatest danger.

You will commonly take notice that boys who lie, very soon show that they are ready for other vices. He, who can so violate his conscience as to tell a willful lie, will soon find it equally easy to violate his conscience by cursing, swearing, or stealing. Indeed, lying and stealing are nearly related. Lying is dishonesty in words; theft is dishonesty in deeds. I know a

Letter 15 — Truth and Falsehood

young man at school who was noted for his disregard of truth. He became a physician, and very soon after was convicted of a very atrocious act of dishonesty. Another was for a long time suspected of no crime but falsehood; it was not long, however, before he was caught stealing the clothing of his friends. Both these were young men of liberal education.

The great reason why we should maintain the truth is, that God requires it of us. "Putting away lying, speak every man truth with his neighbor; for we are members one another."[53] Falsehood is hateful to God. We seem to offer him a direct insult whenever we speak what is untrue, because he is always present, and nothing can escape his omniscience.

Whenever we willfully deceive, we are guilty of falsehood, whatever be the words uttered. Indeed, we may lie without uttering any words at all—by mere signs. We may deceive by being altogether silent; and this is wrong in all cases where others have a right to any information from us. From this you will perceive that all equivocations, or expressions with two meanings, are falsehoods, when the person hearing them understands them so as to be deceived by them. I would earnestly recommend to you to avoid even the very appearance of evil in this thing, and never, even in jest, to sport with truth. It is so awful a thing to

---

[53] Ephesians 4:25.

offend God by a lie, that it is the part of wisdom never to speak what is untrue, even for the purposes of amusement.

I am afraid that young persons at our public schools are too little impressed with the importance of this subject. It is often thought quite a feat when a boy, by a clever falsehood, can escape punishment for a fault; and thus by treating a great sin in a very trifling manner, the conscience becomes seared as with a hot iron. It is alarming to see how readily children learn to depart from the truth, and how hard it is to eradicate the habit. I know people whom I consider pious, but who have never entirely overcome the propensity to stretch their expressions beyond the actual fact. This is what is called *exaggeration* or *hyperbole,* both which words mean about the same; that is, heaping up expressions beyond the simple matter described, or letting our language shoot over the plain truth. Avoid this. It is here, if anywhere, that you are in danger. I cannot believe that you would tell a willful falsehood; but most young persons are apt to exaggerate. Thus, if a servant neglects your horse two or three times, you will perhaps say in anger, "Thomas has forgotten to feed my horse *every day:*" or, "he *never* thinks of feeding my horse." Thus, also, in describing a thunderstorm, some persons always describe it as the loudest and most alarming they ever heard in their lives. This

Letter 15 — Truth and Falsehood

sort of exaggeration is most common among those who have been accustomed to the use of hyperbolical or extravagant phrases in common discourse. Thus some persons cannot speak of a hearty laugh without saying, "He almost killed himself with laughing." Every warm day is the hottest they ever felt; and every ungainly man, the ugliest man they ever saw. Beware of all such unmeaning exaggerations, for you may be assured they lead to the evil habit against which I am warning you.

It is commonly said, and with truth, that great talkers are apt to exaggerate. I hope you will never become noted as a great talker; although I have met with persons who seemed to take a vulgar pride in their very loquacity. "In the multitude of words, there lacketh not sin,"[54] and you will be upon the safe side by repressing your desire to talk. Very loquacious persons commonly talk much nonsense, and, in order to excite attention, sometimes set their invention to work, and give a high color to all they describe. Let me enjoin it upon you, to fix in your mind a sacred reverence for truth; and whenever you describe any incident, take care to describe it precisely as it occurred. Even let your description be flat or cold, rather than run the risk of exaggeration.

---

[54] Proverbs 10:19.

MY BROTHER'S KEEPER

Let your soul be impressed with the awful majesty of God, as being the witness of every word you utter, and you will lose all temptation to violate the truth.

Your affectionate brother,

James

Letter 16

Manly Independence

My dear brother,

The ancients made *fortitude* one of the four cardinal virtues;[55] meaning by this term, not merely the power of enduring pain, but every thing that we now call courage; and they used to say, with truth, that where there was no fortitude, the other virtues were left defenseless. I have often thought that half the bad actions of boys arise from a sort of cowardice, a want of manly independence. Peter will not wear his new hat for several days after he gets it, for fear James will laugh at him. And James, though he knows it is wrong to play truant, does so, lest Charles should think him a coward. In our old-time schools, when we use to "bar out"[56] the master, it was this false shame or lack of

---

[55] The four virtues from ancient Greece: justice, wisdom (prudence), courage (fortitude), and moderation (self-control, temperance).
[56] To exclude or lock out.

moral courage which kept most of the lads from surrendering, even after they had found out that they were in the wrong.

Make it a rule for life to do what you know to be right, no matter what others think or say. Do your duty, and leave the consequences to God. Some people lose their souls from neglect of this. They know very well that they ought to pray, and read the Scriptures, and attend on other means of grace, and own Christ by a public profession; but they are afraid of the scoffs of the world—they hesitate—they procrastinate—they are lost.

Remember, my dear boy, that you are now forming your character for life. When you trained the woodbine[57] around the columns of our piazza, its stock was very slender. You could bend it with your finger and thumb. I looked at it yesterday; it is as thick as my wrist, and perfectly hard and immovable. You might break it, but you could not possibly alter its twists. The woodbine has a habit of being twisted. This habit was formed when it was tender and supple. If it had been trained between long iron bars, I suppose it might have got a habit of being straight. But it is now too late to straighten it. Now, is it not possible that my dear brother is growing crooked? You take my meaning. Is

---

[57] Woodbine is common North American vine with compound leaves and bluish-black berrylike fruit.

Letter 16 – Manly Independence

it not possible that you are getting habits which are wrong? My heart's wish is for you to grow up in such a way as to be erect, upright, and noble, in all your principles. If you are always reckoning what John, or Maria, or this man, or those girls, or the world at large will think of you, it is certain you can never have any manly firmness. I wish you to begin from the hour you read this, to do what is right in every particular case, in spite of what ignorant or wicked youth may say. There is Lewis Lee, your Philadelphia acquaintance. He is altogether a slave to other people's notions. I remember that last summer he refused to accompany his mother to the steamboat, because he had found out that some young gentlemen in Chestnut Street had made free with the cut of his coat.[58] Lewis is not afraid of telling an untruth; but he cannot bear to be the object of ridicule. Again I say, *be independent.* Try to get right opinions, and to do right acts; and bid defiance to idle remark. But be not hasty in forming opinions; be not obstinate in retaining them. Take the advice of the wise and the good, and use every means to learn the best path. Only stick to it when you are sure that you are in it.

Want of this firmness ruins thousands of young men every year. In our colleges, most of the disturbances and rebellions which take place are from

---

[58] To make free meant to make fun or to poke fun at him.

this source. A few youth, who are perhaps already in disgrace, entice a number of others into their plots; and the latter, like silly sheep, follow wherever the ringleaders go. Why? O, because it would expose them to contempt or insult to go back, or return to honorable obedience. They put on a bold face, but they are chicken-hearted in reality. Not one of them can stand alone, or think for himself. These are the lads who grow up to be "men of honor," (that is the name they have for it) duelists, fashionable murderers. O beware of such yielding weakness! "F*ear God*, my children," said a great Frenchman, "*have no other fear.*"

    Your affectionate brother,
James

Letter 17

False Shame

My dear brother,

Long ago I read in one of Miss Edgeworth's tales[59] a maxim which has remained in my memory ever since. It was to this effect: *No one will ever become great who is afraid of being laughed at.* Now I do not wish you to seek after the empty and false greatness of this world. Ambition of this kind is contrary to the mind of Christ. But I desire you to have true greatness, virtuous independence, frankness, generosity, firmness, and decision of character.

It is not necessary for me to spend time in proving to you that the evil of which I speak is very common. Look around among your acquaintances, and you will see many who are more afraid of ridicule than they are of pain. I knew a remarkable instance of this

---

[59] Maria Edgeworth (1767-1849) was a British author who wrote novels marked by clear, vivid style, good humor, and lively dialogue.

fault. *Lucius* was a playmate of mine at school, and a very intimate friend. He was a lad of genius and of many good qualities, but the fear of ridicule was ruinous to him. It spoiled almost all his fine traits. There was nothing so terrible to him as a *laugh.* At any time he would have chosen a whipping rather than a sneer from his school-mates. He therefore was led to do many wrong things, and kept from doing many right things, by his *false shame.* Lucius did not stop to ask whether any particular thing was right or wrong in the sight of God; the first question in his mind was, *What will people think of it?*

The effect of this mental disease was soon manifested, and it showed itself in some ways which were really ridiculous. For example, Lucius became so fully possessed of the idea that everybody was looking at him, and criticizing him, that whenever he walked the streets his whole appearance was affected by it. If he got a new coat, or hat, he was in misery, lest they should draw attention to it. On a certain occasion, I have even known him to walk through a puddle of water in order to conceal the gloss of a new pair of boots. The same foolish pride made him refuse the most useful articles of clothing, if they were a little uncommon. He seemed to imagine that he was an object of universal attention, and was a mere slave to the opinions of others.

Letter 17 — False Shame

Lucius was soon rendered very unhappy; for it was not long before the boys discovered his reigning foible. They took pleasure in laughing at his clothes, his features, his tone, his walk, and almost every thing which he said or did. Poor Lucius could not keep his countenance under their vicious attacks; and sometimes his eyes would fill with tears of mortification. This temper grew up with him, and the consequence is, that he is a poor, feeble, undecided, wavering fellow, who is afraid to take his course with a manly firmness, and must learn the opinion of every one around him, before he ventures upon any proceeding.

This ridiculous pride, or false shame, is something more than a mere laughable peculiarity. It produces real misery, both to the subject of it and to others. Thus many persons are kept from seeking the favor of God by fear of being ridiculed. In like manner, many neglect the duty of professing Christ before men, for the same cause. One young man is ashamed to become a Sunday-school teacher; people will take notice of it, and he will be laughed at! Another young man is afraid to admit that he has religious feelings, or say a word to his ungodly companions, lest they should scoff at him. Thus God is dishonored, and souls are lost.

Read the histories of great men, and you will see how different were *their* feelings. If *John Howard*[60] had regarded those who used to call him "Mad Jack Howard," we never would have heard of his benevolent deeds. Or to go further back, if Columbus had been afraid of ridicule, America might not have been discovered.

Cultivate the habit of doing what is right, come what will. Be firm, be manly; have right opinions, and hold them fast. The dread of idle laughter is the meanest sort of cowardice. Begin at once to overcome it. Especially in matters of duty and religion, beware how you suffer the fear of man to ensnare you.[61] I have known young men who would rather be detected in lying or swearing, than let it be known that they had retired for private devotion. And I have seen boys who would shut their Bible in the twinkling of an eye, and pretend to be doing something else, if any one came into the room where they were reading. How mean, how foolish, how wicked, is such a temper! Scorn to be guilty of this baseness of mind. A proper regard for the opinion of others is surely desirable; but as a rational, an accountable, an immortal being, do not suffer yourself to be in servitude to other minds: above all, do not submit to the paltry laughter of those who are perhaps far inferior in judgment to yourself.

---

[60] See pp. 108-110 of this book for the story of John Howard.
[61] Proverbs 29:25.

Letter 17 — False Shame

I repeat it, then, begin *at once* to conquer this failing, if you are conscious of it in any degree. Do what you believe to be right, in all cases; do it at once, and at all risks. Suppose idle, foolish, or wicked persons laugh at you. What then? Does their laughter injure you? Or will their good opinion repay you for the loss of a good conscience? Is not the praise of God better than the praise of man? You may depend upon it as an undoubted truth, that the very way to avoid mortification is, to despise ignorant ridicule; and the very way to be constantly on the rack of confusion and injured vanity is, to yield to the scoffing of the unwise. And in the things of religion, to be governed by fear of shame is not only foolish, but *impious*. It is nothing less than preferring man to God! Remember the words of Christ: *"Whosoever shall be ashamed of me and my words, of him shall the Son of man be ashamed, when he shall come in his own glory, and in his Father's, and of the holy angels."*[62] Farewell.

Your affectionate brother,

James

---

[62] Luke 9:26.

Letter 18

Evil Speaking

My dear brother,

The sins of the tongue are, perhaps, more numerous than all our other outward offenses.[63] And faults of this kind are very common in young persons. It is not usual to find a youth who is not fond of talking, and where there is much talking, as I have said to you before, there is commonly much sin. Very few boys or girls feel the importance of keeping a strict watch over their lips: and hence, much of their time is taken up in idle, unprofitable, and wicked conversation. I hope I need not say a word more to you about willful lying, profaneness, or slander. These you have been taught to abhor. But there are vices, allied to these, and partaking of their character, into which young persons are very apt to fall. Their wickedness is not so open

---

[63] See James 3:1-12.

Letter 18 — Evil Speaking

and glaring, and therefore they are committed without compunction.

When young people are talking together, in high spirits, nothing is more natural than for them to converse about their neighbors and acquaintances; and they are as likely to speak of the faults, as the excellencies of these persons. In this way, the habit is formed of remarking too freely on personal character, and thus many, before they suspect themselves, fall into the vice of slander. Even when you know of an offence committed by another, it is right to say nothing of it, except where silence would plainly be a sin. "He that covereth a transgression seeketh love."[64] Charity, or true Christian love, rejoiceth not in iniquity—believeth all things—hopeth all things.[65]

In general, the less you talk about absent persons the better. Especially, the less you speak of their faults, the better. Some boys are in a hurry to repeat every thing they hear about the misdeeds of their acquaintances. This shows a low and depraved temper. We may slander, even by speaking the truth; and if we loved our neighbor as ourselves, we should conceal his frailties, just as we always try to conceal our own. The character of a slanderer is justly abhorred. Try to avoid even the appearance of being such. The Scriptures de-

---

[64] Proverbs 17:9.
[65] 1 Corinthians 13:7.

scribe the good man as one "that backbiteth not with his tongue."[66] And they class together "backbiters, and haters of God."[67] In order to keep clear of this vice, beware of *tale-bearing*. There are some things, indeed, which your duty as a son or a pupil will constrain you to make known; and this ought not to be called tale-bearing, but faithfulness.

What I mean to guard you against is the disposition to tattle about every fault or misdemeanor of your playmates or friends. So far as it is practicable or lawful, be the last to carry the bad tidings of a transgression. Be careful not to say any thing about others, which you would not be willing they should hear, or which you would not be willing they shall say of you.

Harsh and reviling language used towards others is a kind of slander. It injures the feelings and the character of those to whom it is addressed. And it is, perhaps, more common among boys than among men; for as persons grow up to years of maturity, they learn the imprudence and the danger of abusing their neighbors with violent words. "Revilers," we are told, "shall not inherit the kingdom of God."[68]

A very common sort of indirect slander is the ridicule often bestowed by the young upon the foibles of their acquaintance. You often hear boys laughing at

---

[66] Psalm 15:3.
[67] Romans 1:30.
[68] 1 Corinthians 6:10.

Letter 18 — Evil Speaking

the peculiarities of some unfortunate youth, and amusing themselves with his looks, his walk, his pronunciation, or his clothes. Where there is a talent for mimicry, this disposition is still more encouraged. Young persons are fond of "taking off" every thing ridiculous in their playmates. Very few persons seem to regard this as wrong; but a little consideration will convince you that it is so; for we always think less of any one who is thus held up in a ludicrous point of view; and this is the very effect produced by slander. The offence becomes a crime when the ridicule is aimed at the natural defects or misfortunes of others. None but the most hard-hearted will sport with the infirmities of the aged, the blind, the crippled, or the poor. And I would advise you to shun the company of any boy who is in the habit of laughing at, or mimicking the natural and unavoidable peculiarities of those around him.

Take care, my dear brother, how you censure the faults of any one. Perhaps you are guilty of the very same. Or, if not, perhaps the report you have heard is untrue. Or, even if it is true, there may be palliating circumstances of which you are ignorant. Or, even at the worst, if it should be all that you might imagine, it can do no good to remark upon it, and you may be inflicting an injury which you can never repair. There is scarcely any thing so dear to man as reputation; and when this is once stained by slander, it is exceedingly hard, and often impossible, to remove the spot.

You are now forming habits for life. I pray you; avoid this habit of evil-speaking. It is one of the most common sins of mankind, and therefore I am the more earnest that you should escape it. Do not even listen to slander. Let all around you know, that it gives you no pleasure to hear your fellow creatures defamed.

Last of all; the surest method of avoiding habits of evil-speaking, is to maintain sincere love for all your fellow-creatures. We never willingly injure those we sincerely love. We never speak bitterly and slanderously of our own dear relations. And so far as we have true charity for all mankind, we shall avoid the very appearance of defamation and slander.

Your affectionate brother,
James

Letter 19

Benevolence

My dear brother,

If I were to send you ten dollars to spend as you choose, after you had purchased such things as you need, what would you do with the remainder? I am sure you would take much more pleasure in giving it to some poor, starving family, than in laying it out upon toys and food. The satisfaction would last much longer. When the miserable sufferers thanked you, it would give you delight; your own conscience would tell you that you had done right; and whenever you thought of it afterwards, it would be with pleasure. But besides all this, there is satisfaction in the very act of doing good. There is something delightful in the very feeling of love.

I wish you to think a little about this. The feeling of which I have just written is called *benevolence,* or good-will. It is the disposition to do good—to make others happy. It is what the Bible calls *charity.* And it always gives pleasure, for we cannot love any one sincerely without feeling a degree of happiness for the moment. Just think of the times when you have felt most affectionate towards your dear parents. Was it not a delightful feeling? And when a kind mother presses her infant to her bosom, does she not enjoy this more than if someone did a favor to her? It is always so. And, therefore, the more benevolent you are, the more happiness you will have. If you wish to be peaceful in your mind, do as much good as you can.

This is a great part of true religion. *"Thou shalt love thy neighbor as thyself."*[69] And wherever this love or benevolence is in any one's heart, it will make him *do good.* He will try to be useful, and to make every one happy around him. Religion begins in the heart, but it does not end there. It leads persons to act. People may talk about religion, and tell how many good feelings they have; but if they never *do good,* if they are not active, there is reason to fear that they have no religion at all. And therefore the Scripture always makes this a mark of true piety. The apostle James says, "Pure religion and undefiled before God and the Father is this: *to visit the fatherless and the widows in their affliction,* and to keep himself

---

[69] Leviticus 19:18; Matthew 19:19; 22:39; Mark 12:31; Romans 13:9; Galatians 5:14; James 2:8.

Letter 19 — Benevolence

unspotted from the world."[70] Is it not a contradiction to speak of a pious man who does no good? You see at once that it is. An idle Christian is no true Christian. We are all sent into the world to honor God, and we do this whenever we perform what is good.

Young persons ought to begin as soon as possible to put this into practice. There is such a thing as learning to do good, and forming a habit of doing good; and we cannot begin too soon. Perhaps you will say that you do not know where to begin. I will tell you. Begin with the very next person you meet; with those who are around you now; with your relatives and your companions. Try to make every one happy to the utmost of your power. Avoid every thing, in your actions, your words, and your very looks, which could give unnecessary pain. Keep this up at all times. Thus you will constantly be cherishing a benevolent temper. If you are kind and affectionate in small matters, I am sure you will be so in those which are more important. There is an old saying about money matters which you may have heard: *Take care of the pence, and the pounds will take care of themselves.* The meaning of this is, that people lose more by neglecting small sums of money, than by losing larger ones. Almost any man will take care of a hundred dollar note. He will carry it in his wallet for months, without losing it. But during

---

[70] James 1:27.

the same time, he will perhaps squander away as much by little and little. If he had taken good care of these small sums, he might have saved a good deal. So it is with respect to benevolence. Almost any man will be benevolent when there is any dreadful suffering which he can relieve, or any great act of charity which he can do. But perhaps this very same man will all the time be unkind and irritable with his family, and will make every one near him feel unpleasantly. But if you begin with these little things, which are occurring every day and every hour, you will preserve a benevolent disposition the whole time, and will be more ready to do some greater act of charity when it is called for.

There have been some men so benevolent, that they have spent almost all their lives in trying to relieve the distressed. One of the most remarkable of these was *John Howard,* who for this reason is usually called *the philanthropist,* that is, the "lover of mankind." Howard was born at Clayton, in England, in the year 1727. His father left him a large estate, but his health was so infirm during his youth, that he did not engage in much active business. He was a man of a kind and tender heart, and was always seeking to do good. When the dreadful earthquake took place which overwhelmed the city of Lisbon, he was so touched with pity that he undertook a voyage to Portugal, in 1755, to see if he could give any relief to the

Letter 19 — Benevolence

inhabitants. But he was taken captive by a French ship, and carried into Brest,[71] where he remained some months as a prisoner. Here he began to learn firsthand how many distresses were suffered by those who are confined in jails, and his benevolent spirit longed to relieve them. When he returned to England he made many inquiries on this subject, and began to examine all the prisons in England, in order to reform them. He wrote books about this, and procured new laws to be passed by the parliament.

But Howard was not contented with lessening the sufferings of prisoners in England. He knew that their case was even worse in other countries, and he determined to visit the continent of Europe. In this work he spent twelve years. Between 1775 and 1787 he went four times to Germany, five times to Holland, twice to Italy, besides visiting Spain, Portugal, Turkey and the north of Europe. He often traveled night and day, visiting all the principal hospitals and prisons. He did not regard expense or danger, for his whole soul was taken up with the desire to do good. At Valladolid, in Spain, he became a prisoner himself for a month, in order to know the real truth of the conditions. And when he returned home, he published a large work, in which he gave an account of what he had seen. And in

---

[71] Brest was the chief base of the Atlantic fleet on the coast of France. At Brest, an elaborate prison was constructed for the galley slaves, implementing the latest ideas in 18th century penology.

this way he did more than was ever done before, to render the condition of prisoners less miserable.

But his benevolent heart was not satisfied with this. The plague was raging in many parts of Europe. This dreadful illness is worse than the yellow fever, and often destroyed thousands in a few weeks. Howard resolved to learn all about it, and find out how it might be cured. He had studied medicine in his youth, and he traveled, as a physician, through various countries. In 1785 he went to Marseilles. Then he visited the hospitals in Italy and Turkey, exposing himself to the greatest dangers. Whenever it was possible, he gave relief. In 1789 he published another work, giving an account of the plague. The same year he set out upon another journey to the eastern countries, but was seized with a fever in the Crimea, and died in 1790.

Now, is not this a noble example? How much more does Howard deserve the name of a great man than Alexander, Caesar, or Bonaparte! I wish you to think of these things, and earnestly to pray that you may be disposed to imitate such a course of life.

Your affectionate brother,
James

Letter 20

Secret Prayer

My dear brother,

The subject about which I intend now to address you is so important, that I might write many letters upon it. It is that of *secret prayer*. I trust that you permit no day to pass, in which you do not pray to God in some secret place.

We are nowhere taught in the Bible how often we ought to pray. It is indeed said that we must *"pray without ceasing,"*[72] that is, that we should all the time be in a fit state of mind for prayer; also that we should habitually observe regular seasons for prayer, and besides, that we should very often offer up petitions in our minds, while we are about our common employments. Almost all Christians have agreed that it is proper to pray to God every morning and every

---

[72] 1 Thessalonians 5:17.

evening. There is a great advantage in having a set time for secret prayer. You have often heard it said, *that what is left to be done at any time, is commonly done at no time.* This is true. If you rise in the morning, and put off your devotions until you feel more in the spirit for them, it is likely that you will be less and less in the right temper. When you become hurried with your studies, your work, or your play, you will be less disposed to pray than when you first arose. Besides, if you have a fixed hour for your private devotions, whenever the hour comes, you will be put in mind of your duty. You know that in a family where the meals are served up at regular hours, every one is reminded of breakfast or dinner whenever the hour arrives.

In a late letter, I spoke to you of the importance of forming proper habits. Now it is one great use of having a stated hour for prayer, that you thus acquire the habit of going into your closet for devotion at a certain time. I remember that I used to have a particular hour for taking a walk in the morning. This became quite a habit with me. Whenever the hour came, I always set out upon my walk, and I used to feel quite unpleasantly when any thing happened to prevent it. So it will be if you set a time every morning and evening for being alone to pray.

Letter 20 — Secret Prayer

It is good also to have a particular *place,* where this is possible. If we go into a room where we have always been accustomed to play and be merry, it will make us think of these things, and we shall be cheerful. If we go into a room where we have seen a person die, it will make us very solemn. What is the reason of this? It is because one thing brings the other into our mind. It is called by philosophers the *association of ideas.* On this account, almost every one feels solemn on going into a house of worship. And in the same way, if you have a particular place where you go to read the Scriptures and pray, you will feel serious whenever you go into it. If it is only a particular corner of your chamber, it will answer a good purpose.

The best time for prayer is early in the morning. As soon as you have washed and dressed yourself, you should go by yourself and engage in devotion. At this hour the mind is fresh and cheerful, and we should give the best hours to God. You are then free from interruptions, and the bustle and hurry of the day have not yet begun. You will naturally be led to think of the goodness of God in preserving you through all the dangers of the night, and it will be highly proper for you to ask his blessing upon the whole day.

The proper time for evening prayer is when the business of the day is generally over. But you must not fix on too late an hour, for in that case you will often be heavy and drowsy, and will hurry through the duty, or perform it in a careless manner. Some thoughtless boys put off their prayers until they have got into bed, and then they pretend to repeat something in the way of devotion. They are afraid to neglect the duty entirely, but they go about it in so slothful a way, that they often fall asleep before they are through their prayers. This is a wicked practice. It is a temptation by which Satan leads many young persons to leave off secret prayer altogether. At public schools, where several boys lodge in the same room, they are often tempted to this neglect. They are ashamed to let their playmates see that they serve God; and this is a dreadful sin. In such a case, it would be a good plan to take an hour before bed-time, in which you could retire to some private place.

Remember that the great thing in prayer is to have the heart right. The words which you utter with your lips are of less importance. You might say over the best prayer that ever was written, and yet if your heart was not in it, you would only be mocking God. Praying is asking. It is asking for what you desire. Now if there is no desire, there is no prayer. If you ask God for things which you do not wish to receive, you are trifling with him, and this is most displeasing to him. Remember also that prayer is heard only for the sake of the Lord Jesus Christ. Therefore, when you

Letter 20 — Secret Prayer

pray, you must have faith in him, or your prayers will not be acceptable. Whenever you kneel down to pray, think what a solemn thing it is that you are about to do. You are going to speak to Almighty God! O, my dear brother, think of this, and you will no longer hurry through your prayers, as if they were some idle tale. Remember the old saying, which is most true: *Praying will make us leave off sinning, or sinning will make us leave off praying.*

Your affectionate brother,

James

Letter 21

The Great Concern

My dear brother,

There are many things to which it is right for you to attend, but there is one thing which is important above all others. It is the *salvation of your soul.* Learning is good, but if you should get all the learning possible, it would only make you miserable, if you were cast into hell. And so it is with every thing else. If, through the blessing of God, you finally get to heaven, it will be infinitely well with you, even if you have been poor and despised, wretched and ignorant.

You know I do not wish you to neglect your learning, but I am very much afraid you will neglect eternal things. This is the true learning; this is eternal life, to know the only true God, and Jesus Christ whom he hath sent.[73] This is what the Bible calls wisdom. A

---

[73] John 17:3.

man may be very learned in worldly things and yet be very foolish. What can be more foolish than to give away eternal joy, to gain a few years of pleasure? This is what many worldly-wise men are doing. *The fear of the Lord is the beginning of wisdom.*[74] A child who is taught of God knows more about divine things than Socrates did.

I am afraid, my dear brother, that you do not think of this as much as you should. I fear that you push away the thought, even when it comes into your mind. This is very dangerous. You may thus harden your heart till it becomes altogether unfeeling. When you turn away your thoughts from religion, you are turning away from God and from Christ. If the Lord Jesus Christ were to come into the house where you live, and show himself to you, just as he did to his disciples at the sea of Tiberias, in John 21, and say to you, *"Follow thou me,"* what would you do?

Perhaps you would say, "I cannot follow Christ now, because I am too young." Many boys say so in their hearts. Christ says to them, *"Follow me,"* just as really as if he were to come into your schoolroom, and take you by the hand, and utter these words. Perhaps you would say, "I cannot follow Christ now, because the boys would laugh at me." Ah, how wicked, how ungrateful is this! The wicked may indeed laugh at you

---

[74] Cf. Job 28:28; Psalm 111:10; Proverbs 9:10; 15:13.

if you follow Jesus. So they laughed at the disciples in olden times. Do you think that the early Christians were free from ridicule? Not at all. They were mocked and scorned wherever they went; and not merely mocked and scorned, they were pursued, imprisoned, and put to death. You cannot follow Christ unless you are willing to suffer for his sake. Are you afraid of the laughter of silly boys and wicked men? Think of the blessed Redeemer. He was not afraid of this, but underwent it, and a thousand times more, to save sinners. People laughed at *him*. They ridiculed him as the *carpenter's son*. They said he was a Samaritan, which was a name of reproach among the Jews. They said he was *mad*. They charged him with having a *devil*. Even when he was working miracles, *they laughed him to scorn*. Yes, and when he was hanging on the cross, in an agony, at the point of death, they wagged their heads at him, and made sport of his blood and suffering. Think of this. This is what Jesus has done for us. And now he says, *"Follow me."* He seems to show you his pierced hands and feet, and to say, "My child, I have borne all this for sinners, and now all I ask is, that you should follow me."

It is your duty, my dear brother, to give your heart to God *now;* to believe *now*. There is no good reason for waiting. All the reasons which come into your mind to make you delay are wicked, selfish,

Letter 21 — The Great Concern

rebellious excuses. *Now* is the accepted time.[75] Tomorrow it will be as hard to believe in Christ as it is today; perhaps much harder, because, as I said, the heart becomes insensible when persons continue to resist the Holy Spirit.

I pray that God would send his Holy Spirit down from heaven, to create a clean heart in you, and to renew you. Your carnal heart is enmity against God, and this is the reason why it is not subject to the law of God. Carnal hearts cannot be subject to the law.[76] And though Christ is every day inviting you, yet you will not come unto him, that you may have life.[77] If you grow up in this state of blindness and impenitence, there is reason to fear that you will become so much the servant of sin, that the evil one will lead you into some open crime. There is a blessed hope of everlasting life given to true believers, and this is what I wish you to enjoy. Perhaps you may not live to be a man. Death sometimes approaches very suddenly. You saw the grave of a little boy not long ago. He was as healthy, a few weeks before his death, as you now are. He had no thought that he was about to die, and now he is in eternity!

Come now, my dear brother, and join with me and your Christian friends in seeking the Lord and

---

[75] 2 Corinthians 6:2.
[76] Romans 8:7.
[77] John 5:40.

calling upon him. "Seek the Lord while he may be found, call upon him while he is near."[78] Make this the chief business of every day, to please God. When you rise in the morning, let your first thought be that you have a soul to save. All the day long, let the salvation of your soul be your principal concern. Other things may wait, without any danger. Your plays and recreations may wait; for if you live, you can attend to them as well hereafter. Your studies may wait, for a few days lost may be regained by diligence. But the *soul's concerns* cannot wait. While you are waiting, death is coming. Death is nearer to you than when you began to read this letter. While you are putting off religion until another day, you are so much nearer to the Day of Judgment. You are loitering and lingering; but time does not linger. And before the day comes on which you mean to begin to seek the Lord's face, your soul may be tormented. O, my dear brother, attend speedily to these warnings. All will be well with you as soon as you are persuaded to follow Christ. Make choice of him—look to him—come to him—receive him—believe on him—and you will at once have the privilege of being one of the sons of God.[79]

Go to some quiet, private place, and tell the Lord in prayer, how great a sinner you have been, and

---

[78] Isaiah 55:6.
[79] Isaiah 45:22; John 1:12; 3:16,18,36; Acts 16:31; Matthew 11:28; John 6:35.

Letter 21 — The Great Concern

mourn over your sin, and cry, "God be merciful to me a sinner!" For "if thou shalt seek the Lord thy God, thou shalt find him; if thou seek him with all thy heart, and with all thy soul." [80] May God abundantly bless you!

Your affectionate brother,

James

---

[80] Luke 18:13; Deuteronomy 4:29.

Other Alexander Titles

Solid Ground Christian Books is delighted to bring back into print *buried treasure* from the Alexander Family of Princeton. In addition to *My Brother's Keeper* now in your hand we are offering the following:

EVANGELICAL TRUTH: *Practical Sermons for the Christian Home* by Archibald Alexander (1772-1851). This volume was produced towards the end of the fruitful life of the man who was called *"the Shakespeare of the Christian heart."* This volume was published to set forth Evangelical Truth in its very essence. The author tells us that the sermons were written to be read within the family circle.

THEOLOGY ON FIRE: *Sermons from the Heart of J.A. Alexander* Joseph Addison Alexander (1809-1860) was a biblical scholar and the third son of Archibald Alexander. Although best known for his classic commentaries on Psalms, Isaiah, Matthew, Mark and Acts, his sermons are masterpieces of evangelical theology on fire.

A SHEPHERD'S HEART: *Sermons from the Ministry of J.W. Alexander* James Waddel Alexander (1804-1859) was the first-born son of Archibald Alexander and especially gifted for the pastoral ministry. Charles Hodge said of him, *"his proper sphere was the pulpit. He was not the first of orators to hear on rare occasions, but the first of preachers to sit under, month after month and year after year."* These sermons were taken from the regular pulpit ministry of the man considered the finest preacher in America.

THE SCRIPTURE GUIDE: *a Familiar Introduction to the Study of the Bible* by James Waddel Alexander is the first in our series of American Sunday School Union Classic Reprints. J.W. Alexander devoted a part of his ministry for over 30 years to the Sunday School Union, writing more than 30 titles for them. Written in the form of a story, the reader is carried along on an unforgettable journey into the realm of Bible Study. Students and teachers alike will be captivated by this resource.

MOURNING A BELOVED SHEPHERD: *Memorial Sermons for James W. Alexander* by Charles Hodge and John Hall. Buried for more than 120 years, this small volume contains the two sermons preached on October 9, 1859 at the memorial service for J.W. Alexander, the beloved pastor of Fifth Avenue Presbyterian Church in NY City. No one can read these addresses without being moved to desire to serve Christ more faithfully. David Calhoun has added a very helpful Preface.

SGCB hopes to reprint several more Alexander titles in 2005 and beyond as the Lord wills. Call us at **1-877-666-9469** to purchase.

Other SGCB Classic Reprints

Solid Ground Christian Books is honored to present the following titles, many for the first time in more than a century:

COLLECTED WORKS of James Henley Thornwell (4 vols.)
CALVINISM IN HISTORY by *Nathaniel S. McFetridge*
OPENING SCRIPTURE: *Hermeneutical Manual* by *Patrick Fairbairn*
THE ASSURANCE OF FAITH by *Louis Berkhof*
THE PASTOR IN THE SICK ROOM by *John D. Wells*
THE BUNYAN OF BROOKLYN: *The Life & Sermons of I.S. Spencer*
THE NATIONAL PREACHER: *Sermons from 2nd Great Awakening*
THE POOR MAN'S OT COMMENTARY by *Robert Hawker* (6 vols)
THE POOR MAN'S NT COMMENTARY by *Robert Hawker* (3 vols)
FIRST THINGS: *First Lessons God Taught Mankind* by *Gardiner Spring*
BIBLICAL & THEOLOGICAL STUDIES by *1912 Faculty of Princeton*
THE POWER OF GOD UNTO SALVATION by *B.B. Warfield*
THE LORD OF GLORY by *B.B. Warfield*
A GENTLEMAN & A SCHOLAR: *Memoir of J.P. Boyce* by *J. Broadus*
SERMONS TO THE NATURAL MAN by *W.G.T. Shedd*
SERMONS TO THE SPIRITUAL MAN by *W.G.T. Shedd*
HOMILETICS AND PASTORAL THEOLOGY by *W.G.T. Shedd*
A PASTOR'S SKETCHES 1 & 2 by *Ichabod S. Spencer*
THE PREACHER AND HIS MODELS by *James Stalker*
IMAGO CHRISTI by *James Stalker*
A HISTORY OF PREACHING by *Edwin C. Dargan*
LECTURES ON THE HISTORY OF PREACHING by *J. A. Broadus*
THE SCOTTISH PULPIT by *William Taylor*
THE SHORTER CATECHISM ILLUSTRATED by *John Whitecross*
THE CHURCH MEMBER'S GUIDE by *John Angell James*
THE SUNDAY SCHOOL TEACHER'S GUIDE by *John A. James*
CHRIST IN SONG: *Hymns of Immanuel from All Ages* by *Philip Schaff*
COME YE APART: *Daily Words from the Four Gospels* by *J.R. Miller*
DEVOTIONAL LIFE OF THE S.S. TEACHER by *J.R. Miller*

Call us Toll Free at 1-877-666-9469
Send us an e-mail at sgcb@charter.net
Visit us on line at solid-ground-books.com

Uncovering Buried Treasure to the Glory of God

Printed in the United States
202809BV00002B/142-144/A